What an amazing book! Karl Clauson writes like he speaks: with passion, clarity, and conviction. I love this book. You'd think a book on killing sin would feel like a heavy weight, when in fact, it's just the opposite. *Killing Sin* is a path to freedom, wholeness, and abundance. This book compelled me to take a deeper look at my motivations and coping mechanisms. I sensed God's holy invitation to believe Him for more, to trust Him on a deeper level. In a world that's quickly normalizing destructive sin, we need this truth-telling invitation to freedom. Bravo, Karl!

SUSIE LARSON
Bestselling author, national speaker, talk radio host

This is a great book. It is provocative, interesting, and convicting. It forces us to finally reject all of our excuses and get serious in the presence of God about "the sin that so easily entangles [us]" (Heb. 12:1 NIV). If you ask me why the church seems so weak today, I would answer it is because we have so many defeated Christians who simultaneously hate their besetting sin and yet find themselves loving to repeat it. This book points the way out of an acceptance of our spiritual doldrums to finally live honestly in the power of the Spirit. Get two copies, one for yourself know who also needs it.

ERWIN W. LUTZER
Pastor Emeritus, The Moody Church, Chica

Sin is ugly. It not only breaks God's law, but our spiritual growth, and it causes pain in our relationships. Sin *must* be killed. In his newest book, Karl does a fabulous job of helping us to know how to win the battle against sin, one choice at a time. He reminds us that "the body of sin might be brought to nothing" (Rom. 6:6) not because of what we do, but because of the power we receive from Jesus Himself. Read this book and, when you are finished, may you long remember that you are "no longer . . . enslaved to sin" (Rom. 6:6).

JANET PARSHALL
Nationally syndicated talk show host

Sin! Consistently, it is the area of the spiritual life that followers of Jesus struggle with most. The persistent sins in our lives can make us mad at our-selves and even frustrated with God. But the Lord is the one who redeemed us from sin and empowers us to live holy lives, if only we'll take advantage of that enablement. And that's where Karl Clauson's terrific book *Killing Sin* can help us all. It is honest, biblical, and practical, giving clear-cut steps to living a life of obedience to God and His Word. Anyone who wants to walk with the Lord Jesus and grow in faith and obedience, don't miss this outstanding and helpful book.

DR. MICHAEL RYDELNIK
Vice President and Academic Dean, Moody Bible Institute; host and Bible teacher, Moody Radio's *Open Line with Dr. Michael Rydelnik*

A must-read for those ready to take a stand against sin! This book leads you on a powerful journey from recognizing the crippling impact of sin in your life to completely uprooting and killing it. You will move from a place of feeling broken and defeated to being energized to fan the flames of the Holy Spirit within you so you can break free to live the life God has called you to. I highly recommend this book to anyone who feels hopeless in their cycle of sin, shame, and repentance and who longs for lasting victory in their war against sin.

ELLEN KRAUSE
Podcast host of *Coffee and Bible Time*

There are countless so-called "remedies" to conquer the ever-present and always-powerful temptation to sin in our lives. But few offer solid biblical solutions. That is why Karl Clauson's book is unique. His approach to killing sin is rooted in Scripture and eminently practical. This book will provide you with life-giving answers to the elusive freedom that you long to experience.

SAM STORMS
Enjoying God Ministries

Which do you want, behavior modification or transformation? Self-help, spiritual whack-a-mole, or empowerment from God? In this book, Karl Clauson gives a life-changing, abundant-life approach to living in freedom.

CHRIS FABRY
Award-winning author and radio personality who hosts the daily program *Chris Fabry Live* on Moody Radio

We live in a culture that's soft on sin. Yet if you don't conquer sin, it will conquer you. What harmful sins threaten to tear your life and family apart? Read this book, not to find condemnation but hope. Karl Clauson will show you that anyone can shake a debilitating habit by hating sin and killing it in God's power. Addressing sin may not be a popular message—but it's a needed one.

ARLENE PELLICANE
Author of *Parents Rising*; host of the *Happy Home* podcast

As we all grow in Christ, we long to experience the shedding of that which encumbers us, but we have to have a battlefield mentality to war through the battle with the power of God's written and spoken word in our lives. Karl Clauson writes with vulnerability, clear biblical instruction, and remarkable clarity on God's desire for our freedom from sin. Be prepared for some precise examination through the loving power of Jesus Christ to call you to experience more in your life as you allow the conviction, confession, and grace of God into your life in a whole new way.

DR. GARY ROSBERG AND BARB ROSBERG
America's Family Coaches; authors of *6 Secrets to a Lasting Love*

My friend Karl Clauson is asking the right question. And for many Christians stuck in a shallow, unsatisfying, and compromised lifestyle it is *the* question. Maybe you're one of them. "What one thing is holding your spiritual life back?" What a fog-cutting question! And I bet in asking it, you can name yours! The real game-changer, however, is not with the question, but in getting a life-changing answer. And this is where Karl is at his best. He offers biblically sound, highly practical wisdom that not only brings freedom but also brings you into a real day-to-day experience with Jesus. I highly recommend it."

ROBERT LEWIS
Founder, Men's Fraternity and BetterMan

We sat down to skim Karl's book for this endorsement but ended up reading the whole thing in one sitting. It is that good! Karl is one of our all-time favorite guests on *FamilyLife Today* because he is a no-nonsense guy who always shoots straight. This book is as straight as it gets. It is time for all of us to "kill sin," and Karl is not only going to motivate you but also give you the goods on the "how." Karl's call to us to get serious about our sin could not come at a more crucial time in our culture. The world is watching, and it is time for us who believe to start living like it. Killing sin is step one.

DAVE AND ANN WILSON
Cohosts, *FamilyLife Today*

Karl reminds us that the reason Christ came was to destroy the works of the devil. We all know the pain that comes when sin is killing us. If we're honest, we all have that one thing that keeps defeating us. It's time to turn the tables on sin and Satan. Sins like anger, addiction, and lust lurk in the shadows, waiting to wreak havoc on our lives. Through the power of God's Word and Spirit we can kill the sin that is trying to kill us. *Killing Sin* isn't just another empty promise ... it is a proven biblical strategy for moving from vulnerability to victory!

CHRIS BROOKS
Senior Pastor, Woodside Bible Church; host, *Equipped with Chris Brooks*

Karl wrote a book about sin that isn't depressing, negative, blaming, or shaming. How is that even possible?! He found a way! Through his compelling stories, many relevant strategies, and brilliant use of familiar and unfamiliar Bible passages and heroes, he has given us a gift. This is a complete teaching on a significant topic we all must embrace. If you've given up on overcoming sin, and who hasn't, this is the book for you. Read it now!

KATHY KOCH
Founder of Celebrate Kids, Inc., speaker, and an author of seven parenting books, including *Parent Differently* and *8 Great Smarts*

As a professor of Bible at Moody Bible Institute, I enthusiastically endorse Karl Clauson's *Killing Sin*. This book provides a solid, spiritually transformative approach to conquering persistent sin in the believer's life. Clauson adeptly weaves together Scripture, personal anecdotes, and practical wisdom to lead readers through the process of identifying, confronting, and overcoming sin through God's power. His emphasis on humility, the work of the Holy Spirit, and the use of God's Word as a weapon against sin is both refreshing and critically needed in today's church. *Killing Sin* doesn't offer simplistic solutions but presents a comprehensive strategy for lasting victory rooted in intimacy with Christ. This book will be an invaluable resource for pastors, students, and any believer serious about pursuing holiness.

JIM COAKLEY
Professor of Bible, Moody Bible Institute; author of *14 Fresh Ways to Enjoy the Bible*

Karl Clauson is one of my heroes. After reading his book *Killing Sin*, he will be one of your heroes too! Karl's message is so refreshingly honest! I mean, who talks about hating and killing sin? That is, other than the Scriptures . . . our Bible is clear—God hates evil, and we should hate it too! Karl goes beyond encouraging us to confess our sins—he tells us how to attack sin, strategically living a life of victory! I love his emphasis on the power of the Holy Spirit and the power of the spoken Word! *Killing Sin* is basically a how-to commentary on Psalm 1, as well as a practical manual for resisting and defeating the enemy. If you're longing for a life of victory, or if you could use some pointers on how to go on the offense in attacking sin, I highly recommend you take the time to read Karl's book.

DAVID NELMS
President, The Timothy Initiative (TTI)

KILLING
SIN

CONQUER THE ONE THING THAT IS DEFEATING YOU

KARL CLAUSON

Moody Publishers

CHICAGO

Scripture quotations are from the ESV® Bible (The Holy Bible, English Standard Version®), © 2001 by Crossway, a publishing ministry of Good News Publishers. Used by permission. All rights reserved. The ESV text may not be quoted in any publication made available to the public by a Creative Commons license. The ESV may not be translated in whole or in part into any other language.

Scripture quotations marked (NIV) are taken from the Holy Bible, New International Version®, NIV®. Copyright © 1973, 1978, 1984, 2011 by Biblica, Inc.™ Used by permission of Zondervan. All rights reserved worldwide. www.zondervan.com The "NIV" and "New International Version" are trademarks registered in the United States Patent and Trademark Office by Biblica, Inc.™

Edited by Connor Sterchi
Interior design: Brandi Davis
Cover design: Graham Terry, Kaylee Lockenour Dunn
Author photo: Claudia Lumperdean

Library of Congress Cataloging-in-Publication Data

Names: Clauson, Karl, author.
Title: Killing sin: conquer the one thing that is defeating you / Karl
    Clauson.
Description: Chicago: Moody Publishers, [2025] | Includes bibliographical
    references. | Summary: "How can we take hold of God's promises and walk
    in freedom-not just for a day or a week but a sustained, lasting
    victory? Karl presents behavioral habits that hold you back, an
    understanding of how change happens, and strategies for winning wars
    grounded in Scripture"-- Provided by publisher.
Identifiers: LCCN 2024031661 (print) | LCCN 2024031662 (ebook) | ISBN
    9780802434593 | ISBN 9780802470751 (ebook)
Subjects: LCSH: Sin. | Change (Psychology)--Religious
    aspects--Christianity.
Classification: LCC BL475.7 .C58 2025 (print) | LCC BL475.7 (ebook) | DDC
    241/.3--dc23/eng/20240807
LC record available at https://lccn.loc.gov/2024031661
LC ebook record available at https://lccn.loc.gov/2024031662

Originally delivered by fleets of horse-drawn wagons, the affordable paperbacks from D. L. Moody's publishing house resourced the church and served everyday people. Now, after more than 125 years of publishing and ministry, Moody Publishers' mission remains the same—even if our delivery systems have changed a bit. For more information on other books (and resources) created from a biblical perspective, go to www.moodypublishers.com or write to:

Moody Publishers
820 N. LaSalle Boulevard
Chicago, IL 60610

1 3 5 7 9 10 8 6 4 2

Printed in the United States of America

To all the people who have the courage to face the sin that's defeating them and dare to believe God can conquer it—Godspeed!

CONTENTS

Going Further

MY STORY—
YOUR STORY

The dream of finishing the Last Great Race came up hollow. I thought there had to be more to life and was dead set on finding it. The chase was on, and nothing would be out of bounds.

We're all reaching out for something or someone to quench the thirst of our soul. The chase for significance and meaning is innate to human nature. Deep within us God gently placed the need to be seen, to belong, and to matter. It's my story—it's your story.

Just three months after completing the 1,100-mile Iditarod trail sled dog race across Alaska in 1979, my life began careening out of control. I put on the happiest face for the next four years, but I was dying inside. Like a car that lost its brakes, I couldn't stop the things I now hated about myself.

I became a slave to my compulsions and addictions. Casual drinking grew into binge drinking. Recreational drug use quickly elevated to panicked calls to dealers as I searched in the night for my next gram of cocaine. They were costing me my health and dignity. Death, in some manner, wouldn't have been far off.

What began as a solution for a hole in my soul left me wrung out and empty. I could drift in and out of most settings without anyone knowing about my demons. I held down a fantastic job in the oil fields, and the work ethic I inherited from my dad made promotions come easy.

But there was a dark side that few could see. Chronic nose bleeds from snorting cocaine and burning my nasal membranes caused me to hide from friends and continue using all alone. My vices shoved me further into a cave of secrecy and isolation.

Soon, common reasoning was gone from my mind. I lived at high risk with zero reward. I didn't want to die, but I didn't care if I lived. When the Feds seized a package of cocaine with my name on it—and I only averted jail time because I didn't pick it up—even that only scared me straight for a week.

Like anyone in the clutches of addiction, I was hopeless and lifeless. I needed something or someone bigger than me to set me free.

"Are You Done Yet?"

On February 11, 1984, while driving somewhere in despair on the cold streets of Anchorage, Alaska, my hopelessness dropped into a deep valley. When I was barely able to catch a break or a breath, the Holy Spirit caught me at rock bottom and called out to me in compassion, "Are you done yet?" Wham! Love broke through.

This shell of a man was ready for love and power. I had a glimmer of hope that what was killing me might be conquered. I turned away from my messy life and gripped God's grace like a safety ring in raging cold seas. I wept on and off for weeks. I loved God's power, mercy, and sweet voice. Shame was washing away, and tears of joy would flow out of nowhere.

It turns out there was more to life. The freedom I found in Christ was relieving, overwhelming, and awe-inspiring. Hope was coursing through my veins. People who knew me well said, "God has changed you completely." I finally knew what Jesus meant when He said, "You must be born again."

On my dad's wise advice, I moved out of Alaska. I was leaving behind destructive friendships and predictable patterns that needed to be broken. I moved in with my close relatives who were genuine Christ followers.

Within days, I was immersed in truth and surrounded by people who could help me take my first steps with Jesus. The strongholds and anchors of spiritual oppression were palpable, but they held no power in my new surroundings.

Freedom was no longer a far-off dream. God had broken me, and my new life in Christ was beginning to grow. What I was chasing had found me.

But soon, I would learn that the battle never ends; it simply comes at us from other directions. If we're not equipped, we'll be unable to conquer what aims to defeat us.

Why I Wrote This Book

It's easy to blame someone or something else when we've made a mess in our lives: friends, colleagues, family, spouses, or a lousy upbringing. Like me, you may have cast blame on Satan, and he, with his ruthless demonic spirits, is a brutal force, no doubt. But ultimately, without taking responsibility for our sin and tapping God's power, we are rendered impotent to conquer anything.

It's crucial to know the three fronts of spiritual conflict. Thomas Aquinas was the first to codify them in his prologue to the commentary on the Apostles' Creed. Three hundred years later, the Council of Trent repeated them, and today, they are commonly referred to as *the world, the flesh,* and *the devil.*

With all its competing values, the world invites us to live for the here and now and neglect investing our lives for eternity. The flesh is our natural tendency to take shortcuts, fall into broken systems of living, rely on ourselves, and settle for less. The devil lures us into believing lies and then delights in hammering us with shame when we take the bait. The world, the flesh, and the devil come at us from all sides. Being aware of them and equipped to stand against them will help us not to get crushed by them.

It was only a short time after those early days of dependence on Christ that I was faced with new battles and giving in to sin that was getting a grip on me. I didn't know anyone who knew how to deal with sin practically as a disciple of Christ. And no one talked about killing sin even though it's a crucial discipline for every victorious follower of Christ.

People spoke vaguely about the spiritual battle and stressed the need for accountability groups, so I joined many. I tend to put up a good front, and soon I suspected I wasn't the only one losing but afraid to admit it. We covered our true selves and resisted sharing just how challenging our raging internal battles with sin actually were.

Accountability groups began as places where people shared vulnerably about an area of their lives that was killing them. The prayers for anyone brave enough to share their battle were thrilling. But without a biblical strategy to conquer what was killing them, most would return to share the failure again, with little lasting success.

Over time, masks replaced vulnerability, causing the group to lose strength. Dwindling and descending into a soft landing, we eventually all moved on. I often wondered if others, like me, experienced more shame for having shared their battles with sin and wished they hadn't spoken up at all. Clearly, we needed a better strategy to allow us to experience long-term victory.

The world, the flesh, and the devil will always be aligned against us. My goal in *Killing Sin* is to share what is evident in Scripture about our battle: (1) there is no peacetime as a disciple of Christ, (2) if we don't conquer sin, it will be killing us, and (3) God has a clear plan for conquering sin. I want to help you identify that one thing holding you back from victory today and God's blessings tomorrow. I want you to hone in on one thing: if you try to tackle everything, you'll be overwhelmed. And my experience is that conquering *the one thing* will be a catalyst for God to conquer other things. My aim is to give you a taste of victory over one big thing, and then you'll have the tools to conquer more.

I wrote this book because, like me, you desire to conquer what's defeating you.

I wrote this book because, like me, you desire to conquer what's defeating you. My story is your story. I will give tested and proven truths from Scripture and teach you how to use them in a way that will cause you to throw off the masks of spiritual pretending once and for all. No longer do you need to hide or suffer alone.

How This Book Will Benefit You

The sin in our lives is paradoxical. We've become desensitized to sin and yet continually suffer defeat from it. We've underestimated sin's consequences, trivialized sin's seriousness, and underinvested in the war against our sin. The sin-shame-repent-repeat madness cycle is not what you have to live with. Your sin can be conquered by hating it, attacking it, and killing it—in God's power.

It's easy to feel paralyzed by the notion that some things will never change. I've known seasons of the sin-shame-repent-repeat cycle of madness. But God can break this cycle. Some sins accelerate physical death while others silently rot our souls, but all sin steals, kills, and destroys (see John 10:10).

Having pastored for many years, I understand that all genuine disciples of Christ have times when they feel defeated and derailed in their discipleship journey. They can't seem to overcome a debilitating sin, an ungodly habit, or a destructive pattern learned from their family of origin. And they feel hopeless about it. If this is true for you, I want you to know this is a shared experience. But God offers hope for you today and a way out.

I have seen the truths in this book radically change my life and the lives of many, and they can change yours too. This book will give you a renewed passion for living. It will help you get honest about what is killing you right now. It will show you how to gain the spiritual power needed to conquer "the one thing" and then go on to conquer other sins.

The topic of this book raises some important questions. Let me answer them now.

- **Why "one thing"?** Trying to tackle everything that needs to change in our lives can be overwhelming and paralyzing. But conquering that one thing can cause other things to topple. All biblical characters struggled with sin, but many battled a particular sin that wreaked havoc. Getting one significant victory through Christ will give you confidence and clarity for other victories.

- **Isn't growing with God a lifelong process?** Lifelong spiritual growth is a privilege of every disciple of Jesus, but it doesn't happen without a fight. Growth is inhibited by sin. Our communication with God can be cut off when sin gets a stronghold (Ps. 66:18). Breaking strongholds of ungodly habits, destructive patterns, and debilitating sin releases us to grow again (2 Cor. 10:4).

- **If I overcome that one thing, what level of freedom should I expect in this life?** We'll never experience total freedom from sin in this life. But the goal is living and running for "the race set before us"—for the same prize of joy that motivated Jesus (Heb. 12:1–2). And to run this race well, we must "lay aside every weight, and sin which clings so closely" (v. 1). If you desire to follow Jesus and take hold of God's promises, you will face adversaries, just as Jesus did. Your battle with sin and evil will go on. This side of heaven, we will never be without sin or a spiritual enemy who wants to trap us in his deception (see John 16:33).

Maybe the most critical question is, "Why can I not seem to break free from my sin?" The feelings of shame, frustration, and defeat are palpable. I've seen a recurring pattern that sets us up for failure: we fully trust God alone to *save our souls* and rely on ourselves to *change our lives.* This book will help you stop trusting in yourself to achieve what you are powerless to do.

Since you picked up this book, I'm guessing you are one of the few unwilling to make excuses for what's holding you back and keeping you down. You want to win. You're unwilling to make any more excuses, and you're done pointing fingers. You're tired of getting

> *I've seen a recurring pattern that sets us up for failure: we fully trust God alone to save our souls and rely on ourselves to change our lives.*

kicked in the gut when you know God promises so much more.

You're dying to live, to finally conquer and kill "the one thing" so you can be lifted, healed, and restored—fully alive in Christ. Every fiber of you aches to distance yourself from something holding you back. Not for a day or a week but sustained conquest—to walk on in freedom and victory—taking hold of God's promises. You dare to believe that nothing is impossible for God.

So, here's where we're going. Like a great symphonic orchestra, there are spiritual movements that capture the heart and lead us to a grand finale—victory over sin! The three spiritual movements I'll be taking you through are as follows:

- **Getting Honest:** Let's peel back everything that keeps you from seeing yourself as you are. This will lead to the breakthrough of identifying, owning, and hating sin. The most remarkable men and women I know are champions of getting honest with themselves and God.

- **Becoming Powerful:** You may have settled for too little—an impotent, sterile relationship with God. Your discovery of where power is born, how power flows, and what happens when power moves will revolutionize your view of God and empower you to kill sin and take hold of God's promises.

- **Killing Sin:** We've been told not to let sin control us but struggle with how to prevent it practically. The strategies for confessing, attacking, and blocking sin will give you tools to finally conquer what's been killing you. No longer will you need to live with the shame of being defeated by the very thing you hate.

Your "one thing," if left to grow and fester, will eat your soul and negatively impact those closest to you. Addiction, gossip, hoarding, laziness, lying, and overeating are just a few of the things that need to be conquered for our sake and others. But here's the crazy thing I've seen: a spiritual domino effect will occur. If you conquer "the one thing," your soul will be restored, you'll gain confidence for inevitable future battles, and you'll spur others on around you. In my experience, a flywheel effect occurs—victory breeds more victory.

Conquering your "one thing" is not out of reach. God is eager and able to radically change your life by breaking your cycles of sin and conquering the things that have seemingly defeated you. When this happens, you'll feel like you found a freshwater stream after walking through a desert.

So, let's get started. Let God fill you up with holy anticipation. But let's first get honest about what's below the surface and capture a grand vision of how God can do what seems impossible. Then we'll learn how to conquer that one thing defeating us!

If you're a leader taking a group through Killing Sin, *I want to help you maximize the experience. Scan the QR code below.*

Download our free
leader's guide here

Nothing Is Impossible

I shall not die, but I shall live,
and recount the deeds of the LORD.

PSALM 118:17

1

A MATTER
OF LIFE
AND DEATH

I n a split second, I went from talking to my wife on my car speakerphone to slamming on the brakes. My world went into slow motion. I was about to T-bone an SUV that ran a red light, and all I could do was brace for impact.

Wham! The collision was intense. Disoriented, I climbed out of my totaled vehicle. Walking through a fog of steam and acrid odor, I went to see how the other driver had fared. Amazingly, he was okay. The adrenaline in my system disguised injuries to my ankle, chest, and hand. Paramedics looked me over and covered a cut, advising me to get anything checked out that might show up later. Within hours, I knew something was wrong with my finger. The painful swelling was a clue to what X-rays showed—my finger was broken.

You will always see the symptoms and feel the pain of what's broken below the surface of your life. Although there may be many things in our lives that need to change, there is often one thing that, if ignored, will hurt us most. Unlike a broken finger, sin never heals on its own.

The One Thing

I host a national radio show from Chicago, *Karl & Crew*. One morning, I told my radio team I had a question I wanted us to ask the listeners. The first question would set up a bigger question. This first question was simple: "What one thing could our Chicago Bears football team change to give them more wins?" It was a painless question for which everybody seemed to have an opinion. Listeners gave many ideas on what to change: owner, coaches, players, offensive schemes, defensive schemes, and even concession selections. If you don't win the Super Bowl, everybody is fair game for blame.

But the bigger question was next: "What is 'the one thing' that needs to change in your life so you can see more spiritual victory and receive God's blessings?" The calls and text responses were overwhelming, and social media comments blew up. They knew "the one thing" in their lives and were ready to share it. I was blown away at the vulnerability and eagerness to share—like the question uncorked their souls.

Here are some direct quotes of the "one thing" listeners identified: poor time management, gluttony, destructive thoughts, rebellion, pride, porn, finances, anxiety, fear, gossip, disorganization, addiction, bad habits, bitterness, apathy, social media, and self.

The deluge of responses was only the first wave. Emails and notes came in for days and weeks as people realized that one thing is holding up everything when it comes to growing strong and gaining ground spiritually.

That morning, God got my wheels turning, thinking about the hundreds of Bible characters who either conquered "the one thing" or were devoured by it. David's sexual sin, Judas' greed, Amon's idolatry, Cain's anger, Peter's arrogance, Simon the magician's passion for power, Sarah's lack of faith, and the rich young ruler's love of money. These are just a fraction of the biblical examples of "the one thing" standing in the way of a breakthrough to victory.

We all have at least one persistent sin that has hurt us, shamed us, or held us back. When asked to pin down that one thing that needs to be conquered, it likely comes straight to your mind. You may identify two or more equally destructive issues, but to secure a victory and not be overwhelmed, just hold on to the one thing that rises above the rest. That one thing is a problem. It stares at you and shames you until you look away or do something about it. Unaddressed, that one thing will diminish us, devastate those around us, or destroy us altogether. And when that one thing persists, it becomes a breeding ground for more things to build up—compromise, denial, and defeat—as we fall under a pile of shame.

But your story is still being written. God can handle your darkest sins and your hidden shame and heal your deepest pain. God's compassion and care are only outstripped by His passion and intention to help you. God can take the most challenging thing you bring Him and conquer it.

We All Start Strong

He started so strong. We all do. With such a head start, you could wonder how he messed it up. He was the kind of guy the women loved, and the men secretly hated. His good looks and stature made it into the Scriptures: "There was not a man among the people of Israel more handsome than he. From his shoulders upward he was taller than any of the people" (1 Sam. 9:2).

A head taller and a head-turner, the people of Israel chose Saul to lead them, and God let them have their way. But Saul had a fatal flaw. He followed God if it suited him. And if it didn't, he went his own way.

Early on, his mentor, Samuel, a godly man, coached him on following God, but Saul soon went off and did his own thing. After conquering several armies and sparing the lives of those who questioned his kingship, he started believing he could do no wrong.

Impatient, self-willed, and wanting to please his fans, he sacrificed to God before an agreed-upon time. It was all for show. He tried to consolidate his power with the people but jumped the gun and didn't wait for Samuel to show up according to God's plan. Then, he fought a battle against the Amalekites, leaving King Agag and the premium livestock alive when God had told him to wipe out everything. He then lied to Samuel by passing the buck and blaming it all on his people.

His excuse to Samuel was he wanted to sacrifice the good stuff to God. But Samuel knew that Saul feared man more than God and loved earthly power more than God's favor. Samuel's response to Saul's lie was epic and relevant to everyone today: "Behold, to obey is better than sacrifice, and to listen than the fat of rams" (1 Sam. 15:22).

Unwilling to obey God and listen to His voice, Saul wore the robes of a king for the rest of his days, but his kingship was already dead—God had moved on and had His eye on David for king.

Saul soon went crazy. Demons harassed him, and only David's merciful strumming on a harp relieved Saul of his torment. Saul's hatred and jealousy of David ate his soul alive. Spending his last years obsessed with killing the king God had now chosen, Saul ignored the rising strength of the Philistines.

In his final battle with the Philistines, Saul committed suicide by falling on his sword. But the shame wasn't over. The Philistines desecrated the bodies of Saul and his three sons. The Philistines paraded Saul's weapons among the Philistine people to raucous cheers. And they hung Saul and his sons' naked, beaten, and beheaded bodies on the wall of Beth-shan.

A handful of men courageously walked through the night to retrieve their fallen leader's body. It was so mutilated, they burned the flesh and preserved the bones to bury their king in honor and preserve the memory of a man who started strong and bright but ended weak and ugly.

How We End Matters Most

This ancient story illustrates a timeless truth: we all start strong, but how we end is the measure that matters most. You started strong; we all do. The new birth miracle of salvation is breathtaking. When you are born again, a whole new life has come, and the old life has gone. You no longer live because the old you died, and Christ lives in you. You have a friend in Jesus, a comforter in the Holy Spirit, and all the power you need to live a godly life.

We all start strong, but how we end is the measure that matters most.

But life goes on. Temptation gives us no rest. The world confines us to broken, impotent systems. And our old appetites can creep back in. When faced with crippling idols and substitute gods that have taken hold of us, we have one thing to do—"be killing sin or sin will be killing you."[1]

Each day presents battles that some don't survive. Like Saul, most of us find ourselves with a flaw that can grow to be fatal, leaving us tormented and stubbornly unwilling to take the way of escape. I know some of the most talented and gifted people who have wrecked their lives by living like Saul. They're still alive, but they have, in essence, fallen on their swords.

When conviction grips your soul, it is a strange blessing. The pain of seeing yourself as you are is the only passageway into richer fields of abundance. John Owen left us with hope in his 1656 classic, *The Mortification of Sin*. "Set faith at work on Christ for the killing of thy sin. His blood is the great sovereign remedy for sin-sick souls. Live in this, and thou wilt die a conqueror; yea, thou wilt, through the good providence of God, live to see thy lust dead at thy feet."[2]

Sin deceives us by making us think that it's not a big deal or that no one will see it. But all sin is a big deal no matter how small the seed you sow. Persistent patterns of sin push us into the shadows of isolation, gnaw at our souls, and steal our joy of walking with Jesus.

I invite you to come face-to-face with God's words, "Do not be deceived: God is not mocked, for whatever one sows, that will he also reap. For the one who sows to his own flesh will from the flesh reap corruption, but the one who sows to the Spirit will from the Spirit reap eternal life" (Gal. 6:7–8).

We will reap corruption if we sow sin and don't kill it, but we will reap life if we sow to the Spirit. A spiritual cost-benefit analysis is clear. The stakes are high. Sin is serious. Romans 8:13 says, "For if you live according to the flesh you will die, but if by the Spirit you put to death the deeds of the body, you will live." Killing sin is a matter of life and death.

KILL SIN—
Reflection and Application

What is that one sin that is killing you?

How would your life change if you finally put it to death?

Romans 8:13 says killing sin is a matter of life and death. How serious are you about killing sin in your life?

Need help identifying your **one thing?**

2

GOD HELP ME!

U nwinnable. That's what you may feel about "the one thing" in your life. But stories of God conquering someone else's "thing" can give you hope and a passionate fire that God can conquer what's defeating you. So, let's start big. Let's look at a story that seems unwinnable for vast swaths of people across America and the world.

With electrodes attached to her forehead, chin, and scalp, the sleep technician told Lori it was time to begin the sleep study. Panic ensued. Memories of abuse as a child and young woman prevented Lori from sleeping, knowing she was being observed. The subconscious threat of harm scrubbed the study before it could begin.

On the walk back to her car, she felt relieved to be out of the room but feared her future. When she told her doctor what happened at the sleep clinic, the response was stark: "Lori, you're morbidly obese; without a sleep study, I can't do the bypass surgery, and without bypass surgery, you're going to die."

Lori's Body Mass Index was hovering around fifty-eight, which is literally off the chart. Her health was beginning to crumble. She could no longer walk down a flight of stairs to wash clothes. Basic movements were limited. Now on medication for diabetes, high blood pressure, high cholesterol, pain, neuropathy, edema, and more, she was facing a certain future; it was only a matter of time, and time was short.

Shuffling to her car from the doctor's visit, she felt the walls closing in and cried all the way home. Back home and desperate, she fell to her knees and cried out to God. "I'm going to die if You don't help me, and I don't want to die!" She went on to get honest with God about the crux of her battle. "God," Lori cried, "my full switch is broken; I can't seem to stop gorging my body. My excuses and my efforts have blinded me. I surrender my body to you. Fix my switch!"

Dying to Live

Deep inside all of us is an innate desire to *live*. We long to experience a robust life that transcends bad habits, addictions, and everyday temptations. We want to overcome aimlessness, discouragement, accusation, and condemnation. These are God-given urges (see Rom. 7:18). Conquering the helplessness of isolation, laziness, repeated failures, and all the other side effects of a broken and fallen world are healthy desires.

God stamped on your soul a passion to thrive—to experience more than humanly achievable and navigate inevitable challenges and setbacks with wisdom, trust, and confidence. You desire to experience deep and abiding love, be freed from condemning words that torment your mind, and no longer rely on cheap substitutes to dull the pain of disappointment.

Thirty-five hundred years ago, a man left a lasting legacy of one thing to avoid at all costs. Korah thought he knew better than God and challenged the leadership of the renowned leader of Israel, Moses—an act of pride that would cost him his life. On cue, the earth shook, and the ground opened and swallowed alive

Korah and 250 co-conspirators.

The cost of pride and the desire for position and prestige would be etched in the memory of Korah's sons. Korah's sons watched their dad die, and they wanted to live. They horrifically saw the price of sin. Korah's descendants were still called "sons of Korah" for at least eighteen generations. The legend of Korah's sin was epic, and for generation after generation, they knew the tragic cost of pride and, in humility, chose life.

The sons of Korah were now worship leaders in the promised land. As good worship leaders do, they helped people then and now get in touch with what they're feeling—what matters most. They wrote a song that reflects the cry of every soul that desires the life of God, fears missing it, and longs for God's protection more than anything. These are the first six verses of Psalm 42:

> As a deer pants for flowing streams,
>   so pants my soul for you, O God.
> My soul thirsts for God,
>   for the living God.
> When shall I come and appear before God?
> My tears have been my food
>   day and night,
> while they say to me all the day long,
>   "Where is your God?"
> These things I remember,
>   as I pour out my soul:
> how I would go with the throng
>   and lead them in procession to the house of God
> with glad shouts and songs of praise,
>   a multitude keeping festival.

Why are you cast down, O my soul,
    and why are you in turmoil within me?
Hope in God; for I shall again praise him,
    my salvation and my God.

Your salvation and your God! The Spirit of God blows like a wind and reaches through the darkness to touch souls and show us in whom life is found, how life is lived when in turmoil, and where to run when our soul is panting with thirst. Our desire to be fully alive is found in God.

Nothing is facing you that God can't knock down. Nothing is mocking you that God can't shut down. And nothing is gripping you that God cannot throw down.

It's All You, God

Lori was dying to live. Kneeling in front of her refrigerator, tears streaming down her cheeks, she sensed something. The hand of God was reaching out to Lori, saying, "Put it all right here; you've carried this far too long. You've tried hard in your strength, and it will never work."

You're never closer to God than when you're at the end of yourself.

As Lori bowed low in a pile of brokenness, Hope knelt beside her. She thought, "Something is truly changing." There was a reason for her optimism: "The LORD is near to the brokenhearted and saves the crushed in spirit" (Ps. 34:18). You're never closer to God than when you're at the end of yourself.

After all the diets, fads, many thousands of dollars, and all the willpower she could muster, Lori would finally experience transformation. God would help her with "the one thing" and change everything. He had crowned her years prior with salvation, and now He would drape another victory over her. But why?

Why in the world did Lori have to get to this point? After many years of following Jesus, I've discovered something you must hear: God can only flex His strength within us when we learn to embrace our weakness. Jesus told the apostle Paul, "My grace is sufficient for you, for my power is made perfect in weakness" (2 Cor. 12:9).

In her spirit, Lori began to hear the Holy Spirit speak through her newly embraced weakness, "That's enough, Lori. You're full enough. Split this entrée with your husband. You're full now, so put the rest away." They were words of unwavering love. Was it up to Lori to respond to the Spirit? Yes. Did she have to come to grips with gluttony being a genuine sin? Yes. But clinging to God with each step of obedience, the Spirit of God guided her into the truth that Jesus, the Bread of Life, is the only One who can fulfill our cravings.

Soon, the Spirit convinced Lori of her need to walk. She could now reflect on the times the Spirit had convicted her to move her body, but her sedentary lazy streak had won the day. Her first walk was one block. Then two. It wasn't immediate, but she could see small wins as she was faithful to walk with God.

Within time, she was walking five miles a day and pressing into God's voice—she was piling up the victories. The temptation never stopped, but God revealed the way of escape as she clung to Him (1 Cor. 10:13).

Today, Lori has lost 175 pounds and sustained it for four years. She has gotten off five medications, and Lori's doctor remains astounded at the transformation. She still has a goal of shedding another twenty-five pounds, and it will happen by God's power alone.

Your "one thing" will either persist in dragging you down and ripping you off, or it will become a catalyst for you to fall in dependence on God, face the truth, hand it to Him, and experience change.

Momentum

Momentum is "strength or force gained by motion or by a series of events."[3] We've all seen the momentum shifts in any sporting event. From the youngest kids' league basketball game to the biggest stages in professional sports—momentum is a game changer. Momentum, although hard to predict and measure, can change a game, a company, a family, and your life.

One small taste of freedom gives momentum for future battles.

The surprising blessing of tackling one thing and getting a win is that it gives you a taste of freedom and momentum for future victories. Conquering that "one thing" isn't always a one-and-done deal. Sin can still resurface and make a counterattack, so we need to be ready to kill it again and keep it subdued by God's power. But one small taste of freedom gives momentum for future battles.

Freedom is contagious and builds momentum for yourself and others. I once saw this while commercial fishing in Alaska. Thousands of dollars' worth of salmon were corralled at the end of our fishing net, and when one fish found a hole just big enough to escape, I watched thousands of fish follow. This is bad news for fishermen in Alaska but good news for you because escaping and conquering is contagious, and you don't have just one thing God wants to change in you. Better yet, others are watching you get wins, and some will want to follow.

There are many layers in the restoration process and victories to be won. But knocking down and conquering that "one thing" is a spiritual momentum builder for future victories and, ultimately, a prize that "will not fade" (1 Peter 1:4).

Lori's victory over her one thing proves that God created us with emotion and momentum, which is a huge asset as we're running to win the prize. God lifted her spirits, unleashed her gifting, and restored vitality to her life so profoundly that Lori is unrecognizable physically and spiritually. The hundreds of people she pours her counsel into through podcasts and life-on-life care are inestimable. Victory leads to victory, momentum matters, and everything changes when that one thing is conquered.

Lift your eyes. Even if you have yet to strike your first blow to what's killing you, keep your eyes on God's promises. Fight the tendency to be swallowed by your sin and failure. Stop all self-effort, worry, and hand-wringing now; it only leads to paralyzing condemnation.

Be sure that "he who began a good work in you will bring it to completion at the day of Jesus Christ" (Phil. 1:6). God has the power to change anything in your life and the will to do it. Ask God right now to give you the faith to believe it!

Redeeming Time

There's truth to the saying, "Idle hands are the devil's workshop." Slothfulness, or being a sluggard, was one of the most common responses to that "one thing" question I asked on the radio. This was a sin that gripped me—too much valuable time was being wasted. I needed to confront it.

Redeeming time does not mean becoming a workaholic; it's about stewarding time wisely as led by the Spirit. Not about working harder or filling every slot in your calendar. Not letting inactivity become a breeding ground for sin.

Many workaholics—and this was my problem—excel at redeeming time in their work lives but neglect time when it comes to their spouse, kids, church, or friends. Redeeming time also involves responding to unexpected needs, getting sufficient rest, and making room for divine interruptions during our day. Watching your grandkids, helping a neighbor load a truck, or even catching a needed nap—in all these and more, God can be glorified.

But many have unredeemed time that gets wasted at the expense of their calling and responsibilities, leading them into traps of temptation. Like me, few people see it, but you know it, and God wants to do something about it.

The Scriptures, particularly Proverbs, are loaded with warnings not to be lazy (see Prov. 6:6; 10:4; 2 Thess. 3:10; 1 Tim. 5:8). Laziness leads to unredeemed time, and Satan is at work to make this a sin in our lives that you and I must conquer. Satan will tempt us with time wasters of everything imaginable and then pound us with condemnation and shame when we take the bait.

You can conquer this "one thing" in your life. Whenever the temptation of laziness is defeated, you'll feel an endorphin rush. Your chin is lifted, and your soul has renewed friendship with God. It doesn't matter if no one sees it. You see it, God sees it, and He's ready to conquer it. And yes, one victory can become a breeding ground for future victories.

The Silver Bullet

That one thing's power to severely damage our lives is real. Some minimize it, others rationalize it, and many compare it to others with "bigger" sins and ignore it. And if you're still wondering what that one thing is for you, I'll soon help you discover that, but for now, you need to know the secret of spiritual success.

So, what causes some people to face that one thing and find a breakthrough while others stay stuck? Why do some people walk free, and others walk in chains when offered the same blessings?

There is a silver bullet for the fatal flaws, crippling habits, substitute gods, and anything else that might be defeating you. It's not easy, but it is simple: *humility*. Humility is the single virtue that sweeps us from the natural realm into the supernatural. As you'll see in chapter 6, humility is where God's power is born.

Humility involves coming face-to-face with yourself, your sins, and any shortcomings and turning to God for help in prayer. Prayer is the engine room of power, and humility is the posture of effective prayer. I'm inviting you into a humble, courageous journey of faith—a trip of overflowing joy, blessing, and overcoming personal failings. But humility isn't what we might think it is. It isn't a flurry of self-loathing or even shedding tears. True humility is looking into the mirror of truth, seeing yourself for who and what you are, and staying there while God is leaning in, ready to help you when you need Him most. Humility is the silver bullet that places yourself in God's hands, knowing He sees it all.

Three Movements

Humility positions you for what I call three vital movements. These aren't "steps" or "principles"; they are the life and art of a relationship with an incomprehensible God who calls us friends. These movements will guide your life to a place of victory, and you can continue moving with Him until the end. Here are the three movements:

1. **Getting honest** with yourself and God.

2. **Becoming powerful** through God.

3. **Killing sin** with three strategies from God.

- Confess it.
- Attack it.
- Block it.

King David, Peter, King Josiah, and the woman at the well are just a few biblical figures who model these transformational movements. God intends for us to conquer that one thing, live well, and be able to help others through spiritual battles.

Each year, on the Fourth of July, the United States celebrates the signing of the Declaration of Independence in 1776. But declaring independence was just the beginning of a bloody battle for freedom. After eleven more years and 50,000 lives lost from combat, disease, and other war-related causes, independence was secured. If the same percentage of people perished in America today, the number would have been 6,840,000 dead.

There is a battleground between declaring spiritual freedom and securing all the freedom Jesus died to give us. We have "been set free from sin" (Rom. 6:7)—declared free. Then, Paul challenges us immediately: "Let not sin therefore reign in your mortal body, to make you obey its passions" (Rom. 6:12)—secure your total freedom.

God didn't send Jesus to give you the gift of new life only to leave you on life support. Conquering that one thing that is killing you is a bloody battle. The following three movements are a battle strategy to win that ground between your declared freedom in Christ and securing all the freedom God has for you.

The world, the flesh, and the devil are brutal enemies of our souls. The battles are real, and feelings of sadness, shame, disgust, or fear are natural responses to sin, but they don't have to define us and leave us in a heap of defeat. The battle belongs to the Lord. Our job is to join Him.

KILL SIN—
Reflection and Application

What practical steps can you take to redeem time and combat laziness?

Dream a little bit: What kind of momentum would be created in your life if you conquered your one thing?

How do you think humility could be a game-changer for you in facing your one thing?

Free devotional series
on **the three strategies**

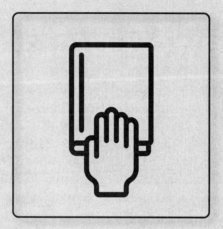

Getting Honest

---

*So whoever knows the right thing to do
and fails to do it, for him it is sin.*

JAMES 4:17

3

FIND IT

Uncover Your One Thing

I was wrung out from sharing my story. It was all about a powerful ministry gone wrong, and the relational fallout was like an atomic bomb. Cleaning up my side of the mess was hard work. I had arranged to meet with anyone I'd hurt, with two others along to witness it, and I did it. It was hard, painful work that caused me to look within myself—owning what you can own in any relationship challenge is critical if you want to walk forward with a clear conscience and the power of God.

The wise counselor who sat across from me gave it to me straight: "You did a piece of the hard work, but now you need to face something bigger." I wondered what was coming. "You have a people-winning problem; it's a cousin to people-pleasing, and it's a sin. You think you can win people without real friendship and without telling the truth." I grabbed a breath, and he said, "Either learn to speak the truth in love, or you'll never have a shot at deep, Godward friendships; you'll only have surface acquaintances."

My leadership style and approach to relating to people were broken. I didn't have a love-and-truth approach. If I saw something that wasn't working, a character flaw, or a blatant sin, I tried to rally people into what I genuinely believed was best for them. In my fear of having honest dialogue, I'd keep trying to win them over without telling them the truth.

Scripture gives us a picture of how to love people in grace and truth: "And we urge you, brothers, admonish the idle, encourage the fainthearted, help the weak, be patient with them all" (1 Thess. 5:14). It may require a straightforward approach for someone who is idle, or a more encouraging and gentle approach for the fainthearted, but everyone needs space to grow.

I learned a harsh lesson: when people-winning or people-pleasing causes us not to share the truth, everybody loses. When my efforts to win them over failed, I'd either work around them or get fed up with them. In either case, people would get hurt. I learned also that some people are super capable but prideful and unteachable. It's not my job to take them on or keep them on as a project, thinking I can do something God can't do until they break.

The damage to myself and others was crushing. The relational shrapnel scarred many. Collateral damage and the lingering effect of relational chaos can be devastating, and we've all experienced it.

Thinking I was loving people by withholding the truth is one of the most significant lies I lived, and it caused me and others never to hear the truth until it was too late. Christ followers must have a good balance of truth and grace—tender words of truth and a willingness to help that person through it. And it's right there in Scripture: "Rather, speaking the truth in love, we are to grow up in every way into him who is the head, into Christ" (Eph. 4:15).

I learned a lot in that season of life, and the Holy Spirit still reminds me how important it is to share the truth and live first and foremost for God's approval.

Call It What It Is

"The presenting problem is not the real problem." The first time I heard this counseling maxim, it struck me as spot-on. Uncovering our "real problem" is the surest way to conquer those "presenting problems." Digging a little deeper, we can find the truth—the real problem.

This is true with that "one thing" in your life. Most of our real problems are below the water line. Like any tree designed to bear fruit, you can bank on this: the stuff that comes out of your life will always be consistent with the root of your life. But be encouraged—God's best work is done in the deep, unseen soil of your soul.

Identifying "presenting problems" and "real problems" is good, but words matter, so let's call things as they are. Sin is humbling and challenging to own, so we have difficulty saying, "I sinned" or "My sin is holding me down." We prefer calling it a problem, issue, bad habit, or weakness. While these descriptors are valid, they can sugarcoat the harsh reality of what we're dealing with—sin.

The biblical term *sin* is derived from the word *hamartia* in Greek or *hata* in Hebrew, which are archery or spear-throwing terms for "to miss the mark" or "flawed." Someone "hamartia-ed" when they did not hit the middle of a target. Identifying where we miss the mark in our lives is virtuous.

As you will soon see, identifying the underlying sin is a work best done by God and with His eyes. The following comparisons are not exhaustive, and I know only some share my struggle with people-pleasing and people-winning. I shared my story to get you thinking about what overarching sin might be holding you back—and what underlying sin might be lurking beneath it.

Overarching Sin vs. Underlying Sin

Pride	Highest authority is not God
Gluttony	Satisfaction apart from God
Greed	Discontent with the generosity of God
Hoarding	Security is not found in God
Lust	Gratification apart from God
Envy	Contentment not found in God
Cowardice	Fear of man more than God
Laziness	Lacking the wisdom of God

The root of all our sins is that something or someone is taking the place of God. When God is pushed to the margins in any area of your life, sin will begin to take root. Self-pleasing and people-pleasing need to be uncovered for what they are—cheap substitutes for God.

The underlying sin can only be seen and dealt with by God. You're more of a humble, broken participant than a frantic, self-willed worker. It's God's work, or it won't work. But the best surprise is discovering that all your exhausting attempts at behavior change are replaced by God, who has all the power and the desire to use it to conquer that one thing defeating you.

If you discover that you've pushed God to the margins in any area of your life, Titus 2:11–12 can help you recalibrate: "For the grace of God has appeared, bringing salvation for all people, training us to renounce ungodliness and worldly passions, and to live self-controlled, upright, and godly lives in the present age."

God's grace saves us and trains us! Your ability to deny what is not of God, to straighten out twisted passions, and to live a life that honors God is all about God's grace. Boiled down, grace is God's power to do in us what we can't do in ourselves.

The best you can bring to God is humble submission and willingness to go God's way. Broken, humble, and reliant on God is the posture of power. No more behavior modification, just readiness and willingness to step out in Holy Spirit power that produces transformation.

We often try to determine what's wrong with ourselves by ourselves. We wind up wringing our hands and maybe asking friends, but they don't have the best view either. Only one person does!

Search Me, God!

King David experienced great victory and great defeat. He also had a rare quality in great leaders—he didn't trust himself. I'm not suggesting that you become insecure or unsure but rather that you put your ultimate confidence in God. This confidence doesn't grow out of nothing. As you'll soon see, it grows by proximity to God. For all the things David got wrong, he got his relationship with God right. The last portion of Psalm 139 is one of my favorite song verses.

> Search me, O God, and know my heart!
>   Try me and know my thoughts!
> And see if there be any grievous way in me,
>   and lead me in the way everlasting! (Ps. 139:23–24)

David invited God to scour his heart and mind and see if his walk was off the mark. Only God can show us what we most need to see. Honest, heartfelt, and believable, David sees God as a friend who will help him, not condemn him.

The voice of God is never heard in the clamor of our striving, but God's whisper is heard at the moment of our complete surrender.

You need what David had: another set of eyes. It would help if you had God's loving look at your life. I invite you right now to take a risk. Get to a quiet place before the day is done. Bring along a piece of paper and a pen. Then, pray David's song. The voice of God is never heard in the clamor of our striving, but God's whisper is heard at the moment of our complete surrender.

Begin to write down what God is showing you. This is the work of the Father, Son, and Holy Spirit. The love of the Father calls out to you. The words of Jesus are held before you like a friend holding a mirror to your life. The Holy Spirit's power guides you into the truth of God's Word and convicts you of what He sees as missing the mark at the root of your life—the real problem.

Our most trusted, efficient, and able counselor is God. We see His mercy, love, and power when we invite Him to meet us at our worst. Let Him search you today. Join God in the work of chasing down underlying sin in your life.

All Cracked Up

The hidden cracks in our lives keep us from living out our full potential and destiny. When I went with my boss to the oil fields of Prudhoe Bay, Alaska, to fix a water treatment plant, we drained a leaking reservoir and found many tiny cracks in the bottom and some large cracks. Pouring epoxy into those large cracks and lightly coating the small ones provided all the water needed for a few hundred workers in the Arctic. We gave special attention to large cracks, and that's what God wants for you as well.

You can pour resources into your life, project the best image, and be perceived as put together, yet you know how frustratingly empty that can be. That emptiness is quickly covered with busyness, substances, or idols without a long-term game.

The best way to improve your quality of life is to let God look for cracks in it and ask Him to heal them. In the book of Jeremiah, God told Israel that they didn't lack provision but that their innermost lives were broken and could hold no water. Broken cisterns, as Jeremiah called them (Jer. 2:13), are deep fractures related to idolatry, lack of integrity, compromised morality, and pride. When God touches and heals your most profound fractures, you strengthen your identity and character. We'll always have hairline cracks, but letting God patch the large cracks will give us the needed momentum to address the smaller ones. With God's help, you will put a finger on your sin. With God's power, He will help heal the cracks in your life. And with God's mercy, He will fill you again to overflowing.

KILL SIN—
Reflection and Application

What overarching sins do you struggle with (see p. 48)?

What fractures of sin do you need God to heal?

What impact could understanding your underlying sin have on addressing your overarching sin?

Need help with
broken systems?

4

OWN IT

Don't Minimize Your Compromise

Recognizing sin is a good thing, but owning it changes everything. Self-protection tempts us to avoid taking responsibility for our sin. We fear retribution, shame, or rejection. Although we've all experienced these at some level, the high road is to own what we can own, knowing that the short-term pain of owning sin is far less than the long-term consequences of not.

Not owning your sins and taking responsibility for them keeps you stuck in a broken system—destructive patterns that confine you to a life that falls short of God's presence and blessings. These patterns may be inherited from imperfect family systems, adopted from twisted worldly systems, or ingrained in us

The short-term pain of owning sin is far less than the long-term consequences of not.

from dysfunctional spiritual systems. But they do not absolve our responsibility.

James Clear wrote in *Atomic Habits*, "You do not rise to the level of your goals. You fall to the level of your systems."[4] This is true in the natural realm of life but best evidenced at the core of our spiritual life. Below are six of the broken systems that I tackle in my book *The 7 Resolutions: Where Self-Help Ends and God's Power Begins*:

- We lack essential spiritual disciplines, so we miss out on hearing the voice of God the moment we most need it.
- We're not mindful of who we are in Christ, so we're easily beaten back into a cave of insecurity and inaction.
- We gather foolish friends around us, so we get pulled down to their level every time we attempt to make changes.
- We stop taking risks, so we've settled for a life guided by mediocrity and the expectations of others.
- We lack focus around our unique calling and gifting, so we find ourselves aiming at nothing and hitting it.
- We don't redeem time, so we see our days swallowed up by others' expectations and squandered by our weaknesses.

However, a seventh broken system is high on many people's lists. Many see this broken system as a lynchpin for tapping God's power.

- We try to manage and cover the tracks of our sin, so our sin winds up managing us and smothering us with shame.

Part of the catalyst for writing this book was the overwhelming response from people who began to experience freedom when sin was no longer rationalized or minimized but put to death—not with self-help but with God's power.

You can clench your teeth and muster all your energy, but nothing releases you from sin like owning it before God. The broken system of not taking responsibility and owning sin is one of the most dangerous. We can only escape the orbit of our sin once we're willing to find it and then own up to it.

Three Ways We Minimize Compromise

When I was faced with my utter failure as a husband, the battle was on. Junanne had just broken through the wall of fear and told me with a quivering chin, "I don't love you anymore." She wasn't angry; she was simply exhausted and honest.

Just seven years into our marriage, waist-high in a powerful ministry and clipping along with what appeared to be a dream family, Junanne revealed how I was missing the mark in one sentence. My sin was not loving my bride as Christ loved the church.

Without words, I walked around a corner and stared squarely into our vanity mirror. The temptation to minimize my compromise was palpable. I could taste my natural desire to list Junanne's shortcomings, and she would have gladly acknowledged each of them.

By God's power alone, I stared at myself as God searched my heart. Then I saw it. In my brokenness, I resisted pride and owned my sin. I wasn't loving Junanne in a way that made her *feel* loved; what she felt was more important than how I thought I was doing.

By God's grace, I owned it without comparing myself to other men I knew who stunk as husbands, blaming Junanne for her part in our glorified roommate status, or listing everything I got right in our home.

We can't minimize our compromise and expect to experience peace with God and others. There must come a time when we see our sin and own it.

Here are three ways we minimize compromise.

1. Comparison: Minimization of sin by comparing yourself with others

You can always find someone worse at life than you, especially when the gauge for comparison is on the surface. The Pharisees were good at this. With circumcised private parts and uncircumcised hearts, the Pharisees compared themselves to others and were the biggest losers.

Jesus blasted their comparison compromise: "They tie up heavy burdens, hard to bear, and lay them on people's shoulders, but they themselves are not willing to move them with their finger.... So you also outwardly appear righteous to others, but within you are full of hypocrisy and lawlessness" (Matt. 23:4–5, 28).

It's so easy to create a gauge for comparison that makes us look good in our own eyes. The comparison compromise is a self-created box by which you compare yourself to others. It is harmful to others but deadly to you—keeping you from owning your sin and taking personal responsibility for what lies within.

2. Blame: Minimization of sin by attaching fault to others

God expected Adam not to eat from one tree. Everything else was fair game. But Adam caved to temptation, and the rest is history and our story.

The Bible records this first blaming compromise. When caught in disobedience, Adam's first response was blame: "The woman whom you gave to be with me, she gave me fruit of the tree, and I ate" (Gen. 3:12). Adam blamed God and Eve in one fell swoop.

Family of origin, our boss, government, spouse, status, kids, birth order, injustice, and God are just a few of the targets we use to pin our sins. There are intensely perceived and self-justified reasons for sin, but no excuses. You've been given a fair shot at the grace of God—that's why it's good news. Adam's blaming compromise got him nowhere, but God helped Adam see what was true, and He does the same for you.

3. Performance: Minimization of sin by focusing on what we get right

Having 90 percent of your life well-ordered can be dangerous. It's easy to count how you got it right when you did. However, performance compromise clouds our ability to see 10 percent of our lives, rendering the other 90 percent less potent and unsatisfying.

A wealthy young man who had his life put together ran up to Jesus and knelt to learn how to get eternal life. He thought he had achieved it. The dialogue between this man and Jesus is remarkable.

> "You know the commandments: 'Do not murder, Do not commit adultery, Do not steal, Do not bear false witness, Do not defraud, Honor your father and mother.'" And he said to him, "Teacher, all these I have kept from my youth." And Jesus, looking at him, loved him, and said to him, "You lack one thing: go, sell all that you have and give to the poor, and you will have treasure in heaven; and come, follow me." (Mark 10:19–27)

Materialism was his blind spot. Unable to surrender his money to God's leadership, he was banking on his performance compromise. But he walked away sad.

God has never turned anyone away for their admitted sins, no matter how bad they may seem. But some, like the rich young ruler, will turn away when they are unwilling to own what they see. Don't let your performance compromise keep you from God's abundance.

Unique Peace

That long look between me and God was brutal. Pride can't co-exist with owning sin. Taking personal responsibility for my failings as a husband to Junanne required me to resist all the prideful ways of minimizing my compromise. What followed was a unique peace, and Junanne and I are best friends to this day.

There is peace for the anxious, the wandering, the worrying, the persecuted, the powerless, and the hopeless. But the most unique peace is reserved for the sinner. "Let us draw near with a true heart in full assurance of faith, with our hearts sprinkled clean from an evil conscience and our bodies washed with pure water" (Heb. 10:22). When we see and own our sin, the unique peace of God clears our conscience and floods our souls.

After three years of witnessing healing, deliverance, and raw power put on display, Peter let the fear of man—more than the fear of God—get the best of him. Peter's denial of knowing Jesus led to one of the most haunting passages of Scripture.

And the Lord turned and looked at Peter. And Peter remembered the saying of the Lord, how he had said to him,

"Before the rooster crows today, you will deny me three times." And he went out and wept bitterly. (Luke 22:61–62)

That quick look into Jesus' betrayed eyes crushed Peter. He had done the very things he hated about others—cowardice and betrayal. He must have wondered how or if he'd come back from this.

But God saw not only Peter's betrayal but also his tears. The good news for Peter, you, and me is that the tears we shed over our sins move God's heart. "I have heard your prayer; I have seen your tears" (2 Kings 20:5).

But God doesn't leave us there. When we see our need for God and own it, our whole mood will shift in short order. "Blessed are you who weep now, for you shall laugh" (Luke 6:21).

Peter must have laughed in amazement that the one whom he betrayed in the face of fear proclaimed him as the rock in the prevailing church (Matt. 16:18). Not a gleeful laugh but a bewildering laugh that God's grace could transform such a sinner.

If you're willing to stop minimizing your compromise and step up to own your sin, your life will change. You'll be surprised at the unique peace within. Don't shrink back at this moment. Look at the sin in your life and own it. You'll be making a big step toward conquering it.

KILL SIN—
Reflection and Application

Which of the seven broken systems do you struggle with the most? How does that affect your walk with God?

Which kind of minimization do you struggle with most?

How would your life be different if you stopped minimizing the sin in your life?

Need help to **stop minimizing sin?**

5

HATE IT

You Can't Kill What You Don't Despise

We drove slowly through the dimly lit streets of Ngozi, Burundi. Shadows of hundreds on foot and bicycles darted in the dark as we drove past. The smells of dinner cooking over open-fire street vendors and the sounds of people in a hurry filled the air. The people of this little-known African country seemed accustomed to living with less.

Shops lit by a single bulb served the working men and women who traded their day's earnings for that evening's meal. In the world's poorest country, people are conditioned to have low expectations—being alive is victory enough.

Burundi, still recovering from a brutal civil war that raged from 1993–2005, is a shell of its potential. The Hutu and Tutsi conflict cost around 300,000 lives, displacing millions and leaving a generation orphaned and in deep poverty. Survival is a way of life; stories of pain and suffering are everyday conversations.

The SUV slowly rounded one last corner, and we arrived at our destination. Our team of four stepped through the light rain into a meeting room. We came to hear the stories of nationals who had survived hunger, abuse, demonization, and injustice. The stories would have been unbelievable if not for the conviction, scars, passion, and tears of those who spoke.

A calmness was over the face of one young man sitting arm's length across a table from me. Then it came time for Viane to share. His voice was steady and unwavering. Everyone in the room was gripped by what we heard.

Viane and his little brother were abandoned by their father at a young age. Their mother, unable or unwilling to handle the pressure of single parenting, soon left as well, leaving the two boys to fend for themselves on the lonely streets of Burundi— two fragile boys, ages seven and five, trying to survive without a family, a home, or love.

Viane's eyes stared off to another place. Viane spoke of a friend who recommended he go to Tanzania to work on a cattle farm. He soon left for a distant place in hopes of richer provisions. With strict instructions, he told his young brother to stay safe and alive until he could return. Viane headed out for opportunity, not knowing he was walking straight into the teeth of more evil.

Viane's arrival at the cattle farm was unfortunate in timing. Valuable cattle began to drop dead, and the owner, unable to prevent the spread of the disease, consulted the local witch doctor.

After summoning the spirits, the witch doctor informed the owner that more cattle would die and that people were next; his family would soon die. There was one solution: discern the person who brought the curse to the farm and kill him. Viane was singled out as the one who carried the curse; he was now destined to be executed.

Viane was called into a courtyard and chained between two trees, arms outstretched for two relentless days without food or water. The witch doctor was suddenly gone. But he would soon return with enough petrol to burn Viane alive.

The Cost of Not Hating Sin

Our anger bubbled up as we listened to what Viane had gone through. Viane's abandoned, hungry, aimless, loveless, lonely life would make any person's heart ache and blood boil. And if you hate injustices like this too, it's a good thing. It means you're human.

This is how God feels about sin. He hates it! He hates what it does to Viane, you, and me. God sees how sin poisons souls and spills onto others, injuring, abusing, and even killing. He knows sin's havoc in our broken world and sent His Son to save us from it. He despises sin, and it's time we get angry about it.

Hate is a lost virtue. From my earliest memories, I was taught not to hate anything. I, and probably you, were told that God is love and that love, not hate, must characterize our lives. But God is not indifferent to or mildly bothered by sin. He hates sin. And we must hate sin too, especially our own.

We should be glad we have a God who has the capacity to love and hate deeply. In the book of Proverbs, we learn about seven sins God particularly hates.

There are six things that the LORD hates,
    seven that are an abomination to him:
haughty eyes, a lying tongue,
    and hands that shed innocent blood,

a heart that devises wicked plans,
    feet that make haste to run to evil,
a false witness who breathes out lies,
    and one who sows discord among brothers. (Prov. 6:16–19)

The cost of not despising sin is that we never have the proper passion to conquer it.

These sins create damage in our lives and those we love. God hates them, and we should too. The cost of not despising sin is that we never have the proper passion to conquer it. Let hatred well up inside you for these sins in your life. The one thing that is killing you may be reflected here somewhere.

- Looking down on others as less than myself
- Lying or shading the truth when it benefits me
- Tearing people down in hopes of lifting myself up
- Planning to take justice into my own hands
- Running to godless things to satisfy the worst in me
- Spreading lies about others to protect my image
- Stirring gossip and division to get people on my side

God hates sin for a good reason. He hates what sin does to erode souls, friendships, churches, and nations. God hates that sin leaves people in bondage, subjects people to abuse, and starves people for love.

Without hatred of sin, we lack the zeal to confront and crush the sin in our lives. Hating our sins is a liberating discovery and fruitful discipline. It's time we got angrier about them—starting with our own. Our natural tendency is to get angry about sin in others—we've felt the harmful effects of their sin in our life. But it's more challenging, humbling, and liberating to hate our own.

Jesus knew our bent to see the flaws in others when He told the story, "Why do you see the speck that is in your brother's eye, but do not notice the log that is in your own eye? Or how can you say to your brother, 'Let me take the speck out of your eye,' when there is the log in your own eye? You hypocrite, first take the log out of your own eye, and then you will see clearly to take the speck out of your brother's eye" (Matt. 7:3–5).

Jesus' words ring true. There's a little hypocrisy in all of us, most pointedly when we can see the sin in others and ignore our own. Own it, no matter how great or seemingly small your sin may be. This takes resolve and courage.

You're Just Not Angry Enough

You may think, "Hey, doesn't God tell us not to be angry?" But Ephesians 4:26–27 says, "Be angry and do not sin; do not let the sun go down on your anger, and give no opportunity to the devil." The anger God tells us to handle carefully is not toward sin in ourselves; it's anger toward others. Anger toward others can allow Satan to influence our lives negatively. But God gives the green light to be angry at our sin.

God's plan has order and progression. We can't love the good without hating the evil. Romans 12:9 gives us a powerful progression in conquering and killing sin: "Let love be genuine. Abhor what is evil; hold fast to what is good." There is a simple three-step progression here that we must see and practice.

1. "Let love be genuine"—For love to be genuine, it must spring from God and sincerely desire another's well-being, seeking their greatest good—which is Christ and a life free from sin.

2. "Abhor what is evil"—This is not merely frowning on sin; it is outright hate. We can't sidestep this. Not hating your sin only prolongs its effects.

3. "Hold fast to what is good"—Hatred of sin frees our hands to grab something better. This is the payoff of hating and killing sin in our lives.

Without hating evil and sin, we find ourselves in a spiritual desert, a place of isolation and struggle. Consider that sin you've been grappling with. It's a formidable opponent. Instead of turning a blind eye to it or downplaying its significance, confront it with a deep-rooted hatred.

God wants to satisfy you! No matter what "the one thing" is that's defeating you, hating it is the correct response. Bring that one thing to mind right now. Whether it's viewing porn, eating way beyond full, looking down on others, being lazy, always wanting more, people-pleasing, or whatever is missing the mark in your life, it's time to hate it.

Sit with it. It's uncomfortable but vital. Don't diminish, justify, or rationalize it—hate it. Despise what that one thing is doing to you. Get animated if that helps. Stomp your feet if you must. Let out a yell, if you will. Hate the impact of your sin on yourself and others, and hate it intensely.

Hate Your Sin, Not Yourself

Viane was going to die at the hands of evil. But God hated what was happening and loved Viane. With his energy and all hope waning, Viane remembered how, as a little boy, he had heard of how a man named Jesus saved people. Viane called out for Jesus to save him in the most desperate moment.

Two days prior, the friend who recommended Viane for this job felt disturbed in spirit and promptly headed to see how Viane was holding up. He walked onto the property at the very moment the witch doctor was on the hunt for petrol to burn Viane to death.

Viane's friend cut him loose. Unable to walk or stand, Viane sank to the soil, listless. His friend quickly hoisted Viane's drained body over his shoulders and began the trip back to Burundi.

Viane's prayer while chained was being answered. God guided him to a man who shared that the Jesus he called out to was real. The fact that Jesus' love could break the chains of neglect and injustice, as well as Viane's sin, was overwhelming.

It would have been easy for Viane to fixate on the sins of others. Victimhood keeps untold millions from facing their own sins. Just before coming face-to-face with the love of Jesus, blind rage was common for Viane. He even threw himself in front of a presidential motorcade and narrowly avoided being gunned down, and just days later, he seriously injured two police officers trying to restrain him. Viane's rage was ravaging his life.

Viane was out of control and in Satan's clutches, and he was a marked man whom townspeople feared. But the prayer prayed in chains freed him from the sins of others and, even better, his own. Viane broke through our natural bent to point outward and looked within. Viane found freedom in Christ—miraculous, thorough, and complete.

Beware of the traps that Satan has set for you. He entices us to look at the failings and cruelty of others so we never look at ourselves. Satan also wants to deceive you into believing the sins of your past and present forever define you. If Satan and his demons, who are whispering lies constantly, can't keep you from heaven, they'll try to hold you in the hell of self-condemnation.

If Satan and his demons can't keep you from heaven, they'll try to hold you in the hell of self-condemnation.

Hating our sin does not mean hating ourselves. Your sin does not define you. It's not who you are. You are a saint who sins—a child of God who can screw things up. Our battle with sin will never end, but no matter how others view you or how you view yourself, what matters most is how God sees us. "Therefore, if anyone is in Christ, he is a new creation. The old has passed away; behold, the new has come" (2 Cor. 5:17). Knowing that your sin is not your identity can launch you into a more robust hatred of sin.

Hating sin is not a commonly discussed discipline of faith, but it's vital for anyone who wants to conquer what is killing them. When you discipline yourself to hate your sin, know this: He is with you, hating it and calling you forward to conquer it. And when you fear God enough to hate your sin and deal a death blow to it, the promise is amazing: "As far as the east is from the west, so far does he remove our transgressions from us" (Ps. 103:12).

A friend shared how God conquered the stronghold of lying in his life. He said the Holy Spirit began to convict him with piercing pain over exaggerating the truth or outright lying to look better. After years of telling untruths, he had developed a seemingly unbreakable habit. He committed before the Lord to correct any untruth immediately after it came out of his mouth.

After a dozen awkward confessions to friends and coworkers, he began to experience the joy of telling the truth. Holding his tongue from fabricating or stretching a story started to kickstart an inner peace he'd never experienced. My friend now has victory.

There will be other battles with sin, but his victory is a testimony in his soul that God can do what seems impossible.

I don't know your sin that's defeating you, but you do. God doesn't hate you for it, but He'll join your hate of it in enabling you to conquer it. All you need is His power to pull it off, and that's what's coming next.

KILL SIN—
Reflection and Application

What would it look like if you truly hated the one thing that is defeating you?

How can you apply Romans 12:9 to the one thing that is defeating you (see p. 65)?

How can you separate your sin from your identity in your pursuit of hating it?

 Free devotional series
on **Romans 12:9**

Becoming Powerful

But you will receive power when the
Holy Spirit has come upon you . . .

ACTS 1:8

6

HUMILITY

Where Power Begins

He leaned slowly back into his chair and offered me his final words. I sensed this would be an essential moment. Everything I'd learned from Robert Lewis for five years had shaped me in ways no formal education could.

We were on our way to God's next assignment. I was asked to be the lead pastor of a hurting church, and we felt called to go. What God would do there would become one of the most impressive displays of His power I'd ever witnessed. Leaving Fellowship Bible Church in Little Rock, Arkansas, where I'd been pastoring for half a decade, and moving my family to Alaska had me gathering all the wisdom I could find.

In addition to all the wisdom I'd gained from Robert about leadership, delegation, and vision, nothing impacted me more than what I was about to hear.

"Karl," he said, leaning forward and reaching to the center of his desk, "when you go to Alaska, there is a secret of leadership I hope you've seen in me, but I've not yet told you." He formed a circle with his hands on the desk and spoke passionately and clearly. "Leadership is like a pie God gives you. Your job is to slice up pieces of the pie and give them away. You'll receive great joy to watch others do things with the slice you gave them that you could never do. But the temptation is to hold back a slice for yourself. Some leaders hold a large slice back, and others just a sliver. But the greatest leaders give away every slice."

With a long pause, Robert smiled. There was more. He reached his right arm into the air. He continued, "Karl, when you've given away every slice of the pie and left yourself with what appears to be nothing"—Robert slowly swung his arm back down to the table like he was holding a new pie on his fingertips—"God will slide you another pie."

It was a moment that I've never forgotten. The lesson was simple: humble leaders eat last but are ultimately well-fed. I strive to live this lesson to this day. I've enjoyed watching my morning radio team thrive with slices of pie. Most were never hired to be on the microphone, but giving them a shot has made everything sweeter, and the pies just keep coming. And the staff at the church I lead in Chicago is thriving—learning the power of giving away what God gave them. Is there a temptation to hold on to a big slice for myself? Sure. But as I hear the voice of the Spirit calling me to give more away and hold on to nothing for myself, the pies keep coming. I get it wrong sometimes, but the taste I've gotten of resisting pride and embracing humility keeps me dishing up what God puts before me. Powerful leaders are humble leaders, and humble leaders eat last.

Worlds Apart

Anyone who desires to conquer sin must learn to reject pride and walk in humility. Pride and humility are worlds apart. Nothing on earth is as pitiful as pride and as beautiful as humility. Pride is the birthplace of all that is evil. Humility is the ground from which all that is good grows. Pride starts wars, but humility makes peace possible. Pride provides the illusion of strength; humility makes the weak truly strong.

> *Anyone who desires to conquer sin must learn to reject pride and walk in humility.*

Humility is not thinking less of yourself. It's not cowering, insecurity, self-hatred, or self-loathing. Pride attributes the best intentions to ourselves and the worst intentions to others. Humility is thinking rightly of yourself and others.

Choosing humility is not an unrewarded exercise of self-denial. The rewards of humbling ourselves are rich. Life, wisdom, and honor are attributes the proud desire and chase but the humble receive. Check out these promised blessings of humility:

Life: "The reward for humility and fear of the LORD is riches and honor and life" (Prov. 22:4).

Wisdom: "When pride comes, then comes disgrace, but with the humble is wisdom" (Prov. 11:2).

Honor: "The fear of the LORD is instruction in wisdom, and humility comes before honor" (Prov. 15:33).

But that's not all. There is another healthy motivator for choosing humility: being exalted by God.

One of Christ's most spirited disciples, Peter, knew how limiting pride was in his life. He also tasted the benefits of choosing to be humble. Peter left us with the most significant promise of humility: "Humble yourselves, therefore, under the mighty hand of God so that at the proper time he may exalt you" (1 Peter 5:6).

Subordination to God leads to exaltation by God. It's not humility motivated by elevation. It's humility motivated by God's glorification and the satisfaction found in Him alone. It longs to be used and poured out by God, whether we're seen or not. To be exalted by God, whether anyone sees us tucked in His hand, is satisfaction enough.

The only way forward when conquering our sins is humility. John Stott, a great theologian, leader, and pastor, said simply, "Pride is your greatest enemy; humility is your greatest friend."[5]

George Müller, the humble nineteenth-century evangelist, lived a life of extraordinary faith and selflessness. Born in 1805, he was the visionary behind the Ashley Down orphanage in Bristol, England—a man who asked for nothing but prayed for everything.

In an era when orphans often had to beg or steal for survival, Müller carved a different path—a humble path. With unwavering dedication, he prayed to create a refuge for these vulnerable children. Over his lifetime, he gave away an astounding $700,000 (equivalent to nearly $15 million today), acquired seven acres at Ashley Down, and spent twenty-one years building homes that would shelter over two thousand children.

His generosity didn't stop there; Müller also funded the printing of thousands of Bibles and paid for countless children's education. But Müller never asked people for money. He bowed low before God and poured out his heart in total dependence. His legacy is a testament to the power of humility.

Where Power Is Born

When you think of spiritual power, you might think of larger-than-life people. You may think of people trained in academia with graduate degrees, a large platform, persuasive personalities, or an enormous following. But spiritual power is not born on a stage, in a seminary, or through social media.

Power is birthed from the humble heart. Power grows in the fertile soil of lowliness. Andrew Murray explains why we can't seem to conquer the one thing defeating us: "Humility is the only soil in which the graces root; the lack of humility is the sufficient explanation of every defect and failure."[6] We have no power without humility.

James 4:6 says, "God opposes the proud but gives grace to the humble." There is no middle ground here. Either God is resisting you and leaving you spiritually impotent, or God is gifting you and making you spiritually powerful.

The posture of humility also has the power to fend off evil forces. "Therefore submit to God. Resist the devil, and he will flee from you" (James 4:7). Submission (humility) before God affords us the spiritual energy to fight a fight that causes Satan and demonic forces to run for the hills.

This is good news for us. It is hope for anyone who feels like their life won't count and that they'll never have the strength to kill what's killing them. Grace is born in humble hearts, and grace packs the punch you need to conquer that one thing defeating you. But grace is not a theory or buzzword. Understanding the full extent of grace has been lost on many.

Training Grace

I exhausted myself for many years. Trying to please God and obey His commands with all my strength, I'd go to great lengths to prove myself to God. Walking deep into the woods one day, I built a fire to show God I meant business. I sat beside the warm flames and told God all the radical things I would do for Him. I built lists in a journal to measure how much Scripture I would read, how much time I would pray, and how well I would perform. I walked out of the woods with more weight on my shoulders than I could bear.

My motivation was almost right, but my method was a mess. All my self-led efforts were a manifestation of pride—thinking I had to take control of my behavior and prove something to God. But pride and self-will left me emptier and weaker.

Grace is the power of God ready to be unleashed in any person who sees their inability and surrenders to God's capability. I had believed there was a saving grace for years. I knew that I had no hand in God saving me from my sin—that was all God's grace and power. But I'd never really known or lived in God's grace and power for growth—that was all on me.

The Bible's most comprehensive working definition of grace is packed into two verses in the book of Titus: "For the grace of God has appeared, bringing salvation for all people, training us to renounce ungodliness and worldly passions, and to live self-controlled, upright, and godly lives in the present age" (Titus 2:11–12).

Look at this grace! It's the power to save *and* train us, to overcome the sin that is killing us. It overthrows our flawed thinking about how to conquer what's defeating us. Many know well that God's power alone saves us and secures our place with God for eternity. But most of us have lived like we need to muster the power to grow in our relationship with God and kill sin in our lives. God's training grace is deposited in our posture of humble submission and empowers us to move the weight of sin.

God's grace is undeserved favor and unreserved power. Understanding this is a watershed moment.

I've wrestled for years with a definition that shows both faces of grace—to save and change us. Simply put, God's grace is undeserved favor and unreserved power. Understanding this is a watershed moment. I hope you grasp it now.

Fully grasp that God's grace gives us the power to say no to the passions that take us away from God. It's grace that gives us self-control. Grace enables us to stand tall and build a life that honors God. The notion that you must be strong enough to kill sin is a lie. Grace alone kills sin. That's why the apostle Paul actually celebrated his weakness. It's counterintuitive to anything we've learned about natural world systems, but it's true, "For when I am weak, then I am strong" (2 Cor. 12:10). Yes, killing sin involves taking severe measures. Exerting effort to kill the sin is difficult. But grace comes first—otherwise, we will labor apart from God's power, unable to do what only God can do.

I was about three months old as a child of God when my dad gave me the best statement about grace I've ever heard. "Karl," he said, "grace isn't the permission to live as we like; grace is the privilege and power to live as we never could before." Get postured for power. The only posture for God's grace and power is humility. Humble people are who God saves, who God trains, and who are fully equipped to kill sin.

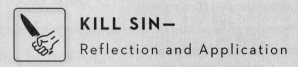

KILL SIN—
Reflection and Application

Who in your life do you know that exemplifies godly humility? What makes their life admirable?

Why is humility so essential to killing sin?

What will it look like for you to practically rely on God's training grace to battle your one thing?

Free devotional series
on **humility**

7

PROXIMITY

How Power Flows

I t was a lazy sunny day in Bristol Bay, but all of that was about to change when we heard screams for help. All the boats were anchored up and waiting for the Department of Fish and Game to reopen the Ugashik district. The tides in Bristol Bay, Alaska, the easternmost arm of the Bering Sea, can swing nearly thirty feet. Every six hours, like clockwork, the ocean fills with rushing water, only to see the rushing retreat six hours later. The sea only stops moving at high water or low—fall into Bristol Bay, and you'll be swept away.

Music was playing onboard our boat, the *Jean M.* I was mending nets, another deckhand was cooking breakfast, and the captain was taking a nap. Screams for help cut the air like a knife. Jumping to our feet, we could see the captain of the boat anchored in front of us, shouting frantically and pointing into the water. The tide was rushing out, and one of his deckhands, Tim, had slipped while working on the boat and fallen into the icy cold waters. You have little time to save a life in Bristol Bay. Get them out quickly, or they'll be lost.

As Tim was now drifting past our boat, we had to save him, or he would die. Captain Marvin, now wide awake, raced to grab a line. He coiled it in his hand and tossed it to Tim, who was panicking, gasping, and barely staying above the surface. Tim reached for it, but it slipped through his hand. We had one more shot. With Tim drifting past our stern, Marvin carefully coiled the line and threw it again. Almost miraculously, it hit Tim's outstretched hand. With one fist, Tim clung to the line with just inches of line to spare. He reached to get a grip with both hands. Tim had a hold on the line, but the work wasn't done.

The ocean didn't want to give him up. As the tide tried to tear the line from his hands, we carefully pulled Tim closer to the boat. We reached down and lashed other lines around his torso as he approached the boat's edge, hoisting him over the boat's port side. Exhausted, shivering, and elated to be safe from the sea, Tim hugged us as we celebrated together—a wild celebration.

As wonderful as this rescue was, there is a rescue that is still greater. We are all born into the outgoing tide of sin. And without intervention, the power and consequences of sin will overtake all of us. But Jesus comes through and throws us the line of salvation. He brings the ultimate rescue by saving us not just from what would end our lives on this earth but from what would destroy us for all of eternity.

The rescue is spectacular whether you are saved early in life or hours before death. Many, like me, were saved after years adrift at sea. As I was living life on my terms and barely treading water, Jesus asked me if I was done fighting to stay afloat and threw me a line. I'm forever grateful.

Perhaps you were genuinely saved at a young age and raised in church. You may think you don't have much of a story, but you do. Whatever the sins in our story—whether addictions, pride, jealousy, selfishness, people-pleasing, or rebellious attitudes—God saves and transforms us all from ugly stuff. Pride, materialism, self-sufficiency, greed, and idolatry—by looking at those in your family, neighborhood, social class, or friends who haven't surrendered to Jesus, you can see the substitute gods you would have adopted or how you would have masked the pain of your soul. Every rescue is radical.

Stay Close

Satan has two main strategies: (1) keep people from seeing their need for salvation, and (2) prevent people from conquering sin and living in victory and abundance. Satan and his demons are actively engaged in deceiving, tempting, and providing fuel to the carnal notion that we don't need God every minute of the day. They want us to be swallowed up by sin without understanding how to walk free.

Remain in the boat and stay close to Jesus! For us who are truly born again into this "living hope," we must remain close to the One who saved us. The only possible way to have a life that counts for something of great good is to stay close to our good God. Sin can cost us dearly in this life, rob others of the impact we could have on them, and limit our rewards on the other side.

The challenge for those of us who have been saved from the powerful tides of sin is this: to remain in the boat and stay close to Jesus. Living in intimate proximity to Jesus will allow us to conquer the most potent sins and bear more spiritual fruit than we could ever dream of!

Jesus used an epic metaphor to teach us how to do this. This metaphor shows how Jesus' power flows through our lives. It's cited in John 15 and contains the most important words Jesus gave His disciples about winning in this life and the one to come. It's so vivid that if you see it in your mind, you'll remember it for the rest of your life. This is what Jesus said:

> "Abide in me, and I in you. As the branch cannot bear fruit by itself, unless it abides in the vine, neither can you, unless you abide in me. I am the vine; you are the branches. Whoever abides in me and I in him, he it is that bears much fruit, for apart from me you can do nothing." (John 15:4–5)

> "By this my Father is glorified, that you bear much fruit and so prove to be my disciples." (John 15:8)

Get the scene in your mind. Jesus is the Vine and holds all the juice and life the branch needs to produce fruit. There are two ends of the branch. One is for proximity to Jesus, the Vine. The other end is for performance and fruit-bearing. You can only focus on one end. If you focus on fruit-bearing, your face naturally has to turn away from your connection with Jesus, the Vine. But if you focus on your connection to the Vine, you will see that fruit flourish one day.

Think about this question: Do you focus more on trying to produce fruit in your life or on proximity to Jesus? Most people I talk with focus on squeezing more love, joy, peace, self-control, etc. out of their lives. But it will never work.

The startling reality is that the further we drift from proximity to Jesus, trying in our strength and ingenuity to produce fruit, the more we drift apart from Jesus and the more susceptible we are to being picked off by sin.

Just take the fruit of self-control. Self-control is not something we are naturally born with. The fruit of self-control that can keep us from caving into sin is only found in proximity to Jesus. When we drift apart from Jesus, we distance ourselves from the only source of self-control that can help us conquer and resist sin. Attempting to produce fruit in our strength and ingenuity is the wrong end of the branch to focus on. You need to focus on proximity to Jesus because that connection will ensure His power will flow through you.

How to Stay Close to Jesus

We've all walked away from a church service, small group, or large conference fired up about something without a clue of what to do. That's what often happens with simple principles of discipleship. We give good information but leave people hanging for how God turns information into life transformation.

But not Jesus. He told us precisely what daily choices will keep us close to Him, and we don't even have to leave the metaphor of the vine and branches. John 15:7 says, "If you abide in me, and my words abide in you, ask whatever you wish, and it will be done for you." And John 15:9 states, "As the Father has loved me, so have I loved you. Abide in my love."

Rest assured, it's all right there! I can guarantee that the distance or gap between you and Jesus will close if you make these three choices.

1. Get the words of Jesus into you. Yes, get into the Word, but the Word must get into you. The way God's Word abides in you is to listen to it at a heart level. But the listening is active. It's being mindful of your life, holding the words of Jesus up to your heart like a mirror, and changing what He shows you. Jesus said the only way to build a strong life is to hear and *apply* truth (Matt. 7:24). Discipleship was meant to be transformational, not informational. This is why listening with a passion for application is the only way to build a life that survives storms. Take baby steps each day. Don't try to tackle too much. Read some of Jesus' words, and when you have something that the Holy Spirit (we'll explore the Holy Spirit more in the next chapter) tells you to apply, find ways to practice it. And that's linked to the next choice.

2. Ask God for His help. This is how we come closer to Jesus as our friend (John 15:15). Asking God for strength in a posture of humility to apply Jesus' words is powerful, and it brings the reality that "Christ in you" is true. Share how much you struggle with your sin in the most accurate terms with maskless honesty. And ask Him for His supernatural power to walk it out with you. God loves to act when we are ready to put truth into action.

3. Enjoy the love of God as you listen and talk with Him. My dad was a good man. He listened to me, laughed with me, told me when I was messing up, and cheered for me when I got wins. God is better at all those things than the best dads. God wants to have a loving friendship with you. I can't imagine how different my life would have been without my dad. He taught me to work hard, rest well, think truthfully, take risks, and how to make changes in my life. God wants to do all of that and more for you. God doesn't hold a scorecard and a whistle. God wants to hold a conversation and help lead you into overflowing joy.

John 15:11 beautifully concludes the vine and branches teaching: "These things I have spoken to you, that my joy may be in you, and that your joy may be full." The pressure is off. Let the power flow, and experience joy in your relationship with Jesus. It's His fruit to produce, not yours. Get your eyes on Him. By continuously clinging to Jesus, we will one day see our lives bearing fruit that blows our minds.

If Christ has saved you, you're safe on the boat, and you are a branch connected to the Vine. Now, the only question is: What end of the branch will you focus on? Performance is exhausting and unfruitful. Proximity pays enormous dividends. The power you desire to have a fruitful life and conquer that one thing is waiting—stay close.

KILL SIN—
Reflection and Application

Have you recently been focused more on trying to produce fruit in your life or on proximity to Jesus?

What choices can you make to live in closer proximity to Jesus?

What is a small, practical first step you can take this week toward living in closer proximity to Jesus?

Free exercise to help you **bear much fruit**

8

LIBERTY

When Power Moves

When I set my eyes on it, I had to have it. It was sleek, fast, made with the latest technologies, and ready to take home for just $499. It was big bucks for a fifteen-year-old in the 1970s, but I had a plan. Liquidating my savings and working out a payment schedule for the balance with my dad and mom, we loaded the Sea Skimmer sailboat into our truck and headed to our home on Lake Lucille.

The next morning, I got up early with nervous anticipation. The wind was strong that day. After raising the mast and lowering the boom, Dad pushed me away from the dock. I had sailed a bit before, just enough to know the basics. Hoisting the main sail and then the jib, I got my first gust of wind. I was off.

It was a rush of adrenaline. The shallow draft hull was built for speed. With the sun beating down, I could feel the harnessed power of the wind pulsing through my little boat and every fiber of me. With the sails full, I was effortlessly skipping across the whitecaps. Soon, our home looked like a speck on the shore. I was going places I'd never imagined with a new sense of power and liberty.

God wants to display that sense of power and liberty in your life. The only hope we have to conquer that one thing defeating us is God's power—full stop! Getting solid on who gives liberty and how power moves through our lives is paramount to killing sin.

My Lost God

The Holy Spirit was my lost God. I can cite reasons for it: I had seen and heard about abuses of the Spirit in some circles of faith, preachers who exploited the Spirit for personal gain, and embarrassing, fake displays of the "Spirit." But none of these were reason enough to neglect or leave out the power of the Spirit's work in my life.

Each person of the Trinity—Father, Son, and Holy Spirit— plays a part in killing sin. And most of us are anchored and together on Holy Spirit essentials: we're saved by the power of the Spirit (John 3:5), sealed and secured in the power of the Holy Spirit at salvation (2 Cor. 1:22), and able to live out the dynamic power and fruit of the Holy Spirit (Gal. 5:22–23). However, I was missing how the power of the Holy Spirit moved in and through my life.

One day, Jesus' words came alive in a fresh way. When He said it was to the disciples' "advantage" that He leave so the Holy Spirit would come—wow! God sent me on a journey to find the advantage I had in the Spirit that I may be hindering. The discovery has been breathtaking, overwhelming, and transforming. I now know that the Holy Spirit is working constantly; if we're not listening to His promptings and voice, we'll miss God's direction and the power we need.

The entire book of Acts is a testimony to the Holy Spirit's power, and He wants to act in that same power today. I have my great-great-grandfather's Bible. Nils Holmbeck loved God deeply. In the back of his Bible, dated April 8, 1886, he wrote, "Listening to D. L. Moody preaching on the power of the Holy Spirit." I turned to the book of Acts, where he had crossed out the heading "The Acts of the Apostles" and written in "The Acts of the Holy Spirit." He was right!

The Holy Spirit's acts are central to the new life in Christ. Paul spoke extensively on the power of the Holy Spirit. Two verses stand above them all. They are God's promises, not a pipe dream. Here's the first:

> Now the Lord is the Spirit, and where the Spirit of the Lord is, there is freedom. (2 Cor. 3:17)

Paul goes on to say that "we are being transformed," and this transformation comes by way of the Spirit. Get this, and don't lose it. Where the Spirit *is*, there *is* freedom! The word translated freedom means "personal freedom from servitude, confinement, or oppression."[7] There is no chain too strong, no sin that has persisted too long, that the Holy Spirit cannot give you liberty from. And here's the other:

> So I say, walk by the Spirit, and you will not gratify the desires of the flesh. (Gal. 5:16)

What a promise! Paul clearly states that the way to prevent sin from defeating us is to walk by the power of the Holy Spirit. You may feel stalled by your sin and afraid you'll never conquer it. But God designed us to walk through life stepping past the desires of the flesh and having the satisfaction of not gratifying them—now that's victory. And the victory is secured by the movement of the Spirit. Understanding how this works must be grounded in the truth of Scripture.

Feel the Power, Stay the Course

The most robust teaching on the power of the Holy Spirit was from Jesus to His disciples. He had just announced His departure, and they were shaken and afraid. Then, Jesus revealed that something new was about to happen, which is for us today.

> "If you love me, you will keep my commandments. And I will ask the Father, and he will give you another Helper, to be with you forever, even the Spirit of truth, whom the world cannot receive, because it neither sees him nor knows him. You know him, for he dwells with you and will be in you." (John 14:15–17)

When they were faced with the news that He was leaving, Jesus reassured them that they would not be lacking in any way. His departure was not a loss but a gain, as it would pave the way for the Helper, the Holy Spirit, to come to them in a new and powerful way. And here is what Jesus told His disciples that forever altered my understanding of the Holy Spirit's advantage.

> "Nevertheless, I tell you the truth: it is to your advantage that I go away, for if I do not go away, the Helper will not come to you. But if I go, I will send him to you." (John 16:7)

This was and is epic, soul-stirring, and encouraging news of inestimable proportions. The disciples then and today are advantaged by the Holy Spirit. Better than having Jesus walk alongside us in the flesh, we have the Holy Spirit who indwells us and gives us the power and liberty to keep us moving in the truth that has been spoken—the truth that gives us freedom over everything, including that one thing that is defeating you.

The Holy Spirit is translated from the Greek word *pneuma*, which means wind or breath. The Holy Spirit wants to fill the sails of our souls. The Spirit gives us the power to move, walk, and run the race. The role of the Spirit is to empower and encourage—to help us kill sin and progress toward fulfilling God's promise of fruit-bearing, overcoming, and walking in victory. One question remains: How does the Holy Spirit move us along practically?

Listen Close

My little sailboat provides a clear metaphor for what Jesus is saying. All sailboats have something unseen that changes everything. A keel goes straight down deep into the water. Mine was about eighteen inches wide and very thin but strong. It's unseen and slices below the waterline. A keel keeps you on course and prevents you from capsizing.

This is why we're called to hide God's Word deep in our hearts— unseen things matter most.

The centerboard represents the truth of God's Word. It goes deep, helping us stay on course and keeping us from spiritually capsizing. Like a keel, the deeper the truth in our lives, the more stable we are in the storms of life. This is why we're called to hide

God's Word deep in our hearts—unseen things matter most.

Jesus doubled down on linking the truth that helps us stay upright and on course with the power of the Holy Spirit. For added emphasis, Jesus calls Him the "Spirit of truth."

> "When the Spirit of truth comes, he will guide you into all the truth, for he will not speak on his own authority, but whatever he hears he will speak, and he will declare to you the things that are to come." (John 16:13)

Notice that Jesus says the Holy Spirit speaks and will declare. He says it twice. For many years as a disciple of Christ, I was unclear how the Spirit brought power to the Word of God. Now it's clear.

Studying Jesus' simple words gave me a new understanding of things I would sense while in conversation with others, driving alone, or lying in bed at night. The Holy Spirit is not inventing new revelation; He is reminding us of all God has spoken by speaking into our conscious minds.

When we are mindful of the Spirit, we will hear Him guide us by reminding us of God's Word. This is why growing in the knowledge of the Word makes us more primed to be guided by the Spirit and reminded of truth when needed.

Raise the Sails

When you discover the vital link between God's Word and the Holy Spirit, you can raise the sails of your soul and be moved to true spiritual liberty, actively conquering sin. As we abide in Christ, the Holy Spirit takes God's Word and empowers us to apply it, bringing transformation—the design God had all along.

The Holy Spirit makes the Word of God alive and active in God's children. The Spirit reminds me to love my wife as Christ loved the church, checks me from gossiping when the opportunity is right in front of me, tells me to look away from temptation so I don't have a hint of immorality, to warn a brother of deadly choices he's making, not to allow a root of bitterness to grow, and to pray for enemies rather than retaliate.

Great women and men of faith have done this for years. But Jesus codified how this works in simple, clear terms: He gave us truth to keep us on course, and we must be powered by the Spirit by listening to Him speak those truths.

This leads to two important takeaways.

1. Get truth deep into your heart. The more truth you have stored up, the more tools the Spirit has to work with. There is truth in the Word for the sin that needs to be conquered in your life. Every temptation you face today is not unique to you, but God has provided "a way of escape" (1 Cor. 10:13). Get the Word into you so the Spirit can help you when you need it most.

2. Be mindful of the Spirit speaking to you. Listening to the Spirit is an advantage. He will guide, direct, and fill you with the power to walk out all the truth you have stored away—the liberty you long for. Raise the sail of your soul. "If you hear his voice, do not harden your heart" (Heb. 3:7–8). Let the power of the Spirit lead you to victory.

The Holy Spirit has all the power to conquer the sin that's defeating you. You might know that sin is killing you, but having the Spirit fill you to put truth in motion is the only way to conquer it. At that moment, when you feel like you have no willpower to fight the battle, the wind of the Spirit can remind you that, in Him, you have all the power you need. God holds out victory before you.

KILL SIN—
Reflection and Application

How have you viewed the Holy Spirit's role in your life? What adjustments might you want to make after reading this chapter?

How can you become more sensitive to the Holy Spirit's voice in your life?

What can you do practically to get more of God's truth in your life?

Free devotional series on
hearing the Holy Spirit

Killing Sin

For if you live according to the flesh you will die, but if by the Spirit you put to death the deeds of the body, you will live.

ROMANS 8:13

9

CONFESS IT

Break the Stronghold of Sin

The Matanuska River rages with silty gray water from mountains and glaciers. It carves its path through a canyon in Southcentral Alaska before pouring into Cook Inlet. Hidden away in the sweeping bends are freshwater streams, where salmon return to spawn, and poachers come to break the law.

One of the toughest men I've known is Mark. Mark, a poster boy for rugged Alaska, had a rebellious streak. He made several trips to the Matanuska River to net salmon and use the eggs for winter fur trapping. But his harvesting of the salmon broke the law, and the hundred or so salmon he took were ninety-seven over the limit.

Mark was recently born again, but as with all disciples of Christ, there can be a gap between what we know to be right and doing it. Mark is about as matter-of-fact as they come. When the Holy Spirit began to speak to Mark, he felt deep conviction that what he did was wrong and that coming clean with state troopers was the right thing to do.

Fear gripped Mark. He had sinned against God and broken the law. He agreed with God that it was wrong, but he didn't

The cost of hiding is steeper than the cost of coming clean.

have the money to pay the considerable fine he would receive, and he sure didn't want the jail time that some had served for similar offenses. The conviction Mark felt to come clean helped him press through the fear. Mark made the call. A trooper said he'd meet Mark at a restaurant to hear him out.

They exchanged greetings, and the trooper listened as Mark confessed. To Mark's surprise, God gave him some unexpected favor. Moved by Mark's genuine remorse, the trooper decided not to file charges. Mark was free to go without a fine or more severe consequences. Overwhelmed with relief and gratitude toward God, Mark continued his relationship with Christ, never poaching salmon again. The fear of consequences, which is common to all, was washed away in the act of confession. Mark's sin lost its stronghold over his life.

Many people hide sin and never confess it. The fear of consequences causes us to hide from man and think we can hide from God. It's true that there may be consequences. God would have been just as good if Mark had to pay a fine or do jail time. But whether it's time served, a fine paid, trust that needs to be rebuilt, or broken relationships on earth, you can't afford to pay the price of a severed relationship with God. The cost of hiding is steeper than the cost of coming clean. It's the hiding of sin that compounds the effects of sin. Some don't hide it—they rationalize, minimize, or try to outrun it. But the stronghold of sin only grows stronger.

Sin feeds in the shadows. It gains strength in the dark. It fights with all the power of hell to never be found out or called out. But the great transfer of strength begins when sin is forced to be known. When we carry our sin, no matter how small or large, to God and others, a supernatural power trans-fer happens. Sin loses its strength when you call it what it is, drag it into the light, hate it for what it's done, and agree with God that it must die.

Sin feeds in the shadows. It gains strength in the dark.

Sin is ugly, painful, and suffocating to your spirit, but it doesn't have to control you any longer. With humility before God, proximity to Jesus, and the liberty of the Holy Spirit, you can break the stronghold of sin.

Come Clean with God

Confession is simply disclosing when we miss the mark and agreeing with God that it's a big problem. It's beautiful when you can lift your head long enough to face God and determine that what He knows is defeating you must be conquered. So many are stalled in their walk of faith, and they know why. Coming into agreement with God by confession is where freedom begins, and sin's power is crushed.

King David knew what it was to be weighed down and waste away under his sin. But he also knew how to get out from under the soul-crushing pounding of condemnation.

James Montgomery Boice describes how much one of David's songs impacted the great theologian and philosopher Augustine of Hippo: "This was Saint Augustine's favorite psalm. Augustine had it inscribed on the wall next to his bed before he died in order to meditate on it better."[8]

Blessed is the one whose transgression is forgiven,
    whose sin is covered.

Blessed is the man against whom the LORD counts no iniquity,
   and in whose spirit there is no deceit.
For when I kept silent, my bones wasted away
   through my groaning all day long.
For day and night your hand was heavy upon me;
   my strength was dried up as by the heat of summer. *Selah*
I acknowledged my sin to you,
   and I did not cover my iniquity;
I said, "I will confess my transgressions to the LORD,"
   and you forgave the iniquity of my sin. *Selah* (Ps. 32:1–5)

Here are two takeaways from David's words in Psalm 32:

1. The consequences of sin are real. Unique to those who fear God is that the things we used to blow right past make us nearly stop dead in our tracks. The painful awareness that we've missed the mark with God impacts the totality of who we are—body, soul, and spirit. The consequences of sin are real. King David lost a son and destroyed two families over his lust. We always reap what we sow unless God offers unusual grace. But some consequences of sin are universal—they apply to all sins, small or large. David's experience is our reality as well.

Sin can make us feel God's hand: God's love compels Him to press in on us when we sin. We "groan" in our sins because God loves His children enough to put the full weight of His "heavy hand" on us and compel us to come clean. This happened to David, and it probably is happening to you. But God's passion is our restoration.

Sin can make us physically sick and weak. Some sickness, though not all, is related to sin. David's sin made him feel like his body was "wasting away"; this strong man's strength was "drying up" from a spiritual fever. This is why James 5 says there is healing when sin is confessed to God before the elders. Even physical affliction can be used by God for spiritual restoration.

2. The blessings of confession are potent. David gives us a vision of richness and reward for confessing our sins to God. Many have underestimated the potent blessings of confession, and Satan aims to keep them hidden. Holding on to these two epic prizes of confession can motivate you to agree with God about your sins.

God covers what we couldn't cover up: He "covers our sin" and separates it from us "as far as the east is from the west" (Ps. 103:12). The very thing we wanted all along happens. The sin we tried to hide, disguise, or diminish is now invisible to God by His choice. God so covers our sins with forgiveness, it's as if they never happened.

God wipes clean the sin we couldn't see. When our "spirit has no deceit," the scoreboard is reset to zero. God is faithful to scrub our souls and "cleanse us from all unrighteousness" (1 John 1:7–9). No matter how much Satan may accuse us, our confession of sin leaves no marks against us.

David sinned in horrible ways, committing adultery with Bathsheba and plotting for the death of her husband to cover up his sin. A child was born and tragically died as a result. David's sin and attempts to cover it up was a royal mess, but a redeemable mess. No sin has taken you beyond the reach of God. You're never too far gone. And the best move to make right now is confessing that one thing you know is robbing you of an abundant and victorious life.

True Confession

Confession of sin isn't without pain. Erwin Lutzer speaks to confession's difficulty: "Forgiveness is always free. But that doesn't mean that confession is always easy. Sometimes, it is hard—

incredibly hard. It is painful to admit our sins and entrust ourselves to God's care."[9] The pain comes from a wounded ego, bruised esteem, and staring at the pain of your failure, wondering how you got here. But remember, you are not stuck in your sin. Confession, though difficult, brings a sense of relief and liberation, paving the way for spiritual healing.

God's Word is designed to be acted on. He never leaves us wondering what to do or how to do it—He wants you to get results. Here are four basic confession tactics that will give you immediate results.

1. **Drag "the one thing" into the light.** There may need to be a more focused intent on dealing with one thing. It's easier to deal with lesser things to make us feel better about ourselves without tackling "the one thing" holding you back from spiritual victory and receiving God's blessings. Do it now. Don't let it hide any longer. God is big enough to handle your deepest, darkest sins.

2. **Confess your sin to God by agreeing with Him and doing whatever it takes to correct wrongs.** Speak out about what sin you need God's power to conquer. Call it by name. Don't soften or diminish it. Describe it to the God who already knows it. Confession to God is like a dam breaking—what was held back can now flow. Remember, the blessings of God's forgiveness are too profound to miss out on. His love and mercy are always there, ready to comfort and reassure you.

3. **Confess your sin to a trusted friend or spiritual leader.** Confession to a trusted friend or spiritual leader (James 5) is God's way of putting teeth into confession. There's something about someone in the flesh hearing our

heartfelt admission of sin that brings camaraderie and steals power from Satan, who thrives on secrecy. Find a trusted friend or leader and pour out your heart.

4. **Celebrate that the stronghold of your sin is broken.** Celebration is a must. You don't need to do time in a penalty box. There is no need to feel sullen or pay penance. The price for your sin was paid at the cross.

When we cover our sin, God reveals it; when we confess our sin, God covers it.

When God looks at you, He sees the righteousness of His Son. Here is something worth celebrating: when we cover our sin, God reveals it; when we confess our sin, God covers it. Celebrate the love of God, who sees you for who you are and loves you still. The victory over sin is yours to celebrate, bringing joy and uplifting your soul.

After David explains the power of confession in Psalm 32, he has another verse of the song that captures the overwhelming joy of confession.

Therefore, let everyone who is godly
offer prayer to you at a time when you may be found;
surely in the rush of great waters,
they shall not reach him.
You are a hiding place for me;
you preserve me from trouble;
you surround me with shouts of deliverance. *Selah*
(Ps. 32:6–7)

David compares confession and forgiveness to a military con-quest. The shouts of deliverance are what David felt in his heart when he experienced the retreating of torment in his soul. This is for you as well. When you think your battle with sin cannot be won, God gives you victory. Confession is a lost discipline that you can reclaim as your own. It's a weapon of spiritual war that you can no longer neglect. The relief you'll experience through confession lifts the heavy load you've been carrying so you can walk and even run with Jesus again.

KILL SIN—
Reflection and Application

Have you ever experienced the joy of confession? What were the effects on your life?

What keeps you from confessing your sins to others?

To whom can you confess the one sin that is defeating you?

How can you celebrate the stronghold of "the one thing" being broken?

Free eBook on
confessing sin

10

ATTACK IT

Put Sin to Death

I was staring at a defeated man. His wife had just caught him using porn. She was crushed, he was ashamed, and they were both wondering where to go from here. He had made repeated pledges to God and himself that he'd never watch porn again. Failing to keep his promises, his secret sin was ultimately discovered.

Brandon (not his real name) had tried everything. He was a strong man who had never faced another challenge he couldn't conquer. So he thought he could leverage his strength to conquer pornography, but he just kept failing. No amount of grit, resolve, or repeated vows to himself and God seemed to change a thing, and in different seasons, the porn use would get worse and darker.

Behavior modification had failed him—it always does. There he sat, rudderless, helpless, and lifeless. And that was the root! The power of God had saved Brandon, but he had never moved on to discover the great adventure of living in that power. His lust was taking root in a soul that lacked gratification in God.

It can feel overwhelming to conquer lust, fantasy, pornography, or any other "thing" that's defeating you. Brandon's attempts to change his behavior were as futile as any of our attempts to conquer sin with grit, willpower, or resolve.

But something flipped. Brandon began attacking pornography in the way you're about to see and is now walking free. He has no appetite for pornography compared to the truth of who he is in Christ. He is walking the road less traveled. His wife battled to trust him, but over time, Brandon's consistency in Christ and letting God's work be the proof of profound change have freed her from bitterness and inspired her to discover her one thing.

Any effort to conquer that one thing in your life without God's power and plan will make you think you're destined to be a failure. This is the greatest lie Satan tries to pull on God's kids. All human efforts to manifest good in our lives leave us in a heap of exhaustion, embarrassment, and shame—convinced our battle will never be won.

Kill What's Killing You

Killing sin might not be a common topic in conversation, but it needs to be. Puritan writer John Owen famously wrote, "Be killing sin or sin will be killing you."[10] Either sin dies, or you die, but one or the other will die.

We discuss sin, resolve to fight sin, find accountability for sin, get counseling for sin, and deal with sin in ways that end up leaving the sin intact and us in pieces. Being held accountable or getting counsel around you is fantastic. But all of this needs to come to the "Y" in the road of deciding to put sin to death and finding a strategy for doing it.

All sins, no matter what yours may be, are insidious and debilitating. Gossip destroys reputations and trust, overeating destroys health and longevity, slothfulness destroys productivity and esteem, and addictions of all kinds destroy individuals, families, and communities. Killing sin is war, and Jesus got graphic in defining it:

We discuss sin, resolve to fight sin, find accountability for sin, get counseling for sin, and deal with sin in ways that end up leaving the sin intact and us in pieces.

"If your hand or your foot causes you to sin, cut it off and throw it away. It is better for you to enter life crippled or lame than with two hands or two feet to be thrown into the eternal fire. And if your eye causes you to sin, tear it out and throw it away. It is better for you to enter life with one eye than with two eyes to be thrown into the hell of fire." (Matt. 18:8–9)

Jesus uses hyperbole to make a crucial point: attacking sin at the source is necessary. Take extreme measures to kill what's killing you, or it can cause great spiritual harm. Don't play with or try to manage it; put it to death. This is where the battle is most fierce.

When it comes to putting sin to death, John Piper explains, "There is a mean, violent streak in the true Christian life! But violence against whom, or what? Not other people. It's violence against all the impulses in us that would make peace with our own sin and settle in with a peacetime mentality."[11] The peacetime mentality needs to end now! The Bible is clear about how to handle sin. We must attack it with an intensity that will leave it without breath.

- "Put to death, therefore what is earthly in you: sexual immorality, impurity, passion, evil desire, and covetousness, which is idolatry" (Col. 3:5).
- "So you also must consider yourselves dead to sin and alive to God in Christ Jesus. Let not sin therefore reign in your mortal body, to make you obey its passions" (Rom. 6:11–12).
- "And if your foot causes you to sin, cut it off. It is better for you to enter life lame than with two feet to be thrown into hell. And if your eye causes you to sin, tear it out . . ." (Mark 9:45–47).
- "For if you live according to the flesh you will die, but if by the Spirit you put to death the deeds of the body, you will live" (Rom. 8:13).

If you're struggling with people-pleasing, jealousy, ungratefulness, pride, self-righteousness, addictions, or any other sin, there are ways to put these to death, and we must get about killing sin, or sin will be killing us.

Porn was killing Brandon, so he had to get honest about where he was vulnerable and what he had to do to kill that sin in his life. No matter what sin you are conquering, make time to get honest about the circumstances and situations that feed the beast of sin.

Dangerous Downtime

Gordon MacDonald noted that unseized time flows to our weaknesses. It's true! The most dangerous time for compromise is idle time. You can have nothing but focus throughout your day and feel productive, fruitful, and satisfied in Christ. Then, you have a break in the day, get home, and have an hour with nothing much to do. WHAM! Every possible compromise—what we eat, where we scroll, and what we watch—sneaks up on us and grabs us by the throat.

Brandon realized that he was most tempted to scroll for porn when his time was unclaimed. Satan loves unclaimed time. For Brandon, it meant programming his phone to shut down access to apps or servers after work and making scrolling for porn impossible. From overspending to mindlessly wasting time or diving into dark compromises, putting limits on devices is just plain practical and fruitful. Sin is at our fingertips like never before in history, but God knows the time and place we're in, and He can deliver us from evil.

As Brandon surrendered his downtime and other vehicles of compromise to God, he found victory in ways he could not have imagined for many years. More time for reading and talking with his wife and getting to bed on time were just a few of the hidden blessings. If the Holy Spirit prompts you to put limits on devices, don't wait. Whatever the Spirit guides you to do, take that advantage and work on it now. God is at work in you.

How Sin Dies

I've counseled a few people who didn't want to kill sin in their lives, and it never ended well for them. But genuine Jesus followers can't stand living with what's killing them. They want to conquer it. We can see how serious God is about putting sin to death. We can have a deep passion and resolve to conquer sin but wind up landing right back in the same sin all over again—the sin-shame-repent-repeat cycle must end now!

There is one sure way to kill sin. I can assure you that just as confession breaks the power of sin, there is one thing that can put sin to death—the spoken Word of God. The Word of God cannot only be pages in a book, locked away in the crevices of your mind and never acted on; it must be spoken out, or sin will survive.

Speaking truth is not some magical incantation; it's agreeing with God and proclaiming the truth with spiritual authority. Jesus said, "If you abide in my word, you are truly my disciples, and you will know the truth, and the truth will set you free" (John 8:31–32).

We must speak truth to our sins from a heart of humble submission to God. This is biblical, practical, and powerful. Speaking truth to kill sin involves two strategies, often neglected and rarely utilized in the church today: (1) muttering God's truth out loud and (2) directly declaring God's truth to that sin to put it to death. The former is a way of living in ongoing abundance; the latter is putting a direct hit on that one thing defeating you.

1) Mutter God's Truth

When you see men at the Wailing Wall in Jerusalem rocking back and forth, something from the book of Joshua is going on. If you step up close to them, they are muttering (wailing) or speaking God's truth aloud. Although these Jewish men don't see Jesus as the Messiah and they lack the transforming power of a relationship with Christ, they are fulfilling a discipline that's clear in Scripture and underutilized by us today.

When Joshua was about to take the nation of Israel into the promised land, God told him how to overcome enemies, avoid sinful idolatry, and have "good success."

"This Book of the Law shall not depart from your mouth, but you shall meditate [*hagah*] on it day and night, so that you may be careful to do according to all that is written in it.

For then you will make your way prosperous, and then you will have good success." (Josh. 1:8)

The Hebrew word for meditate is *hagah*, which means "to mutter, growl, utter, speak, or muse." Meditation is not an exercise to be played out in your heart and mind alone. And it's certainly not emptying our minds to let whatever thoughts invade it. Today people are emptying their minds and leaving them wide open for Satan and demonic forces to fill that void with twisted truth and lies. Biblical meditation involves "hiding God's word in your heart" (Ps. 119:11) and "renewing your mind" (Rom. 12:2), but it is so much more.

Biblical meditation, the kind God intended, was to mutter and rehearse the truth of God's Word—repeating aloud what we know so that we will have spiritual success. The power of words is real. "Death and life are in the power of the tongue, and those who love it will eat its fruits" (Prov. 18:21). When we speak or mutter God's living and active Word, our life imitates God's words and becomes fruitful.

The word *hagah* is used in my favorite psalm. This song starts with our common challenge—hanging out with the wrong people and what to do about it so they won't drag you down.

> Blessed is the man
>   who walks not in the counsel of the wicked,
> nor stands in the way of sinners,
>   nor sits in the seat of scoffers;
> but his delight is in the law of the Lord,
>   and on his law he meditates [*hagah*] day and night.
> He is like a tree
>   planted by streams of water

that yields its fruit in its season,
and its leaf does not wither.
In all that he does, he prospers. (Ps. 1:1–3)

There it is again! Look at the benefits of *hagah*. You won't be influenced by the chatter of the wicked, sinners, and scoffers and get wrapped up in their mess, but you will mutter God's Word and prosper. What a huge blessing to meditate on the Word of God!

2) Declaring Truth to Sin

Words matter. Two Greek words define God's inspired Word. Both are transformational, but one is used to battle evil. *Logos* means the Word of God, and *rhema* means the spoken Word of God. We've often neglected *rhema* because some have used it to wield their own words and declare them as God's words. Any counsel or words claiming to be from God must align with Scripture, or it's heresy.

But *rhema* is the spoken word that God has already declared in His Word—all the truth we need to attack sin and finally put it to death. God has given us an arsenal of His words to be used as weapons of war. We first see this word when Satan tempts Jesus to sin.

"Man shall not live by bread alone, but by every word [*rhema*] that comes from the mouth of God." (Matt. 4:4)

While being tempted by Satan, Jesus modeled the power of speaking God's Word to knock evil back on its heels. Jesus spoke Scripture back to Satan and his deceptive twisting of truth. It's not a magic trick; it's an assertive discipline that deals a blow to evil.

Paul teaches the church how to get armored up and fight Satan, thereby winning daily battles over sin. He uses the same word and imagery as the battle with temptation Jesus fought.

> And take the helmet of salvation, and the sword of the
> Spirit, which is the word [*rhema*] of God ... (Eph. 6:17)

The sword of the Spirit, the Word of God, is our only offensive weapon of war. All the other parts of the armor are vital: the belt of truth, the breastplate of righteousness, the shoes of the gospel of peace, the shield of faith, and the helmet of salvation, but wielding the sword of the Spirit is how enemies are killed.

Without using the Word of God as our offensive weapon of war, it's like sending an army to battle with full body armor, but no guns—the enemy never dies. The sword can fend off the enemy's attacks and the sin to which he tries to chain us. *Rhema*, God's spoken word, is how we can conquer sin. Declaring God's Word to sin is the most powerful way to put it to death.

The Spirit of God reminds us of truth, and we wield that truth in agreement with the Spirit. This is why raising the sails of your soul and listening to the Spirit to give you direction is vital. He will prompt us when we need to battle sin, and speaking truth to sin will deal an actual death blow to sin.

Mining the truth of God's Word to battle the sin you face in the Spirit is paramount. In the "Going Further" section at the back of the book, I've included a starter guide for many areas of sin and corresponding truths to declare after you confess the sin and are ready to put it to death.

In my experience, declaring truth to temptation and sin is a tragically underutilized weapon of spiritual war. Getting God's Word in your hand, heart, or mind is good. Memorizing verses related to your specific sin and other everyday battles is better. Declaring those truths as guided by the Holy Spirit is best. God's

Word neutralized Satan and caused him to leave when Jesus spoke it out to him. And your sin, when confronted with spoken truth, will lose its power too. I know this personally because it's a common practice for me that gives victory. God's Word is authoritative and powerful. Know it, memorize it, and wield it well.

KILL SIN—
Reflection and Application

What do you tend to do with unseized time? How can you better leverage this time for God's purposes in your life?

What extreme measures can you take to kill what's killing you?

What specific promises can you speak over yourself to kill that one thing in your life? (Refer to the Starter Guide on p. 135.)

Practical ways to
kill specific sins

11

BLOCK IT

Place Boundaries to Prevent Sin

We had a big moose problem. It all started with me wanting to treat my bride to something special. We had a nice little area in front of our townhome in Anchorage, Alaska. The raised, contoured plant bed was great for flowers but lacked a centerpiece. One day at a nearby nursery, we found it: a Snow Fountains Weeping Cherry Tree. It stood about four feet tall and would only grow a bit more. It was costly, like investing in a piece of furniture. But when summer came the following year, it would have beautiful white blossoms.

It never made it! I was having an early morning coffee when I first saw them. Two towering moose were eyeing the leaves of my bride's special gift. Knowing they eat almost anything with life in it, I ran back to the nursery and got a bottle of repellant spray. After spraying the tree, I thought we were safe. But rounding the corner coming home the next day, two huge moose had the tree cornered, and they were chomping away like it was a little appetizer—the spray must have just been a pleasant seasoning. I laid on the horn, and they scampered off. The weeping tree still had some life, so it was time for something more. I ran back out to the nursery and picked up some chicken wire. I built a cute little perimeter fence around the now sobbing tree and, again, thought we were good.

A week went by, and I felt we were in the clear. After a short trip away with the family in our little motorhome, our joy sank as we rounded the final corner home. I stopped the motorhome just in front of the tree. All four of us sat stunned as we gazed through the windshield at the aftermath of destruction. The moose must have laughed at the chicken wire. It lay stomped on the ground with the easily accessed tree devoured. All that remained was a four-foot-tall stick. Every single branch had been stripped off—nothing was left. The tree and our dreams for the following spring were dead.

To add insult to injury, a couple of months later, my bride was taking our kids to school. I had just left, keeping the garage door up because they'd be leaving shortly. When they opened the hallway door to the garage a couple of minutes later, a giant moose greeted them. His ears were pinned back, very angry to be disturbed. After rearranging things on my workbench, he soon turned to walk out, stopping just long enough to drop a big load on my clean garage floor. I learned over a couple of months that if I was going to guard myself and my family from a moose invasion, I'd need boundaries—good ones!

We Need Boundaries

A boundaryless person provides unfettered access to forces that want to consume their life. Not everyone or everything is aiming to devour you, but without boundaries, you won't know until it's too late. We need boundaries—firm, solid, reliable boundaries. Boundaries are discussed throughout Scripture.

- God set boundaries in the creation that we enjoy today. "And God said, 'Let there be light,' and there was light. And God saw that the light was good. And God separated the light from the darkness" (Gen. 1:3–4).
- Jesus had boundaries to get time alone with the Father. "He would withdraw to desolate places and pray" (Luke 5:16).
- Paul tells us to set boundaries about what floods our minds. "Finally, brothers, whatever is true, whatever is honorable, whatever is just, whatever is pure, whatever is lovely, whatever is commendable, if there is any excellence, if there is anything worthy of praise, think about these things" (Phil. 4:8).

Sin intends to eat away at our lives. It's no light matter; the most valuable things are destroyed by sin. We can't allow sin unencumbered access to our lives. Nor put ourselves in places that make it more likely for sin to kill us. Good boundaries provide spiritual protection.

You want to conquer sin, and setting solid boundaries is central to doing that. Boundaries are not impenetrable walls; they are buffers between yourself and potential risk factors that afford you the time and space to assess danger and make wise, thoughtful decisions that could be the difference between life and death.

The more proficient we become at blocking sin, the less we will need to kill it. Establishing healthy boundaries is essential to building a life that is not devoured by sin. Blocking sin is a proactive move to fend off specific attacks. It's a spiritual preemptive strike.

God established and taught us healthy limits, which are an enormous blessing. They fall into three main categories: moral boundaries, relational boundaries, and spiritual boundaries.

The rewards of having these boundaries are another powerful lesson from the first three verses of Psalms.

> Blessed is the man
> who walks not in the counsel of the wicked,
> nor stands in the way of sinners,
> nor sits in the seat of scoffers;
> but his delight is in the law of the LORD,
> and on his law he meditates day and night.
> He is like a tree
> planted by streams of water
> that yields its fruit in its season,
> and its leaf does not wither.
> In all that he does, he prospers. (Ps. 1:1–3)

God packed three boundaries into three verses: delighting in the law of God; getting distance from the wicked, sinners, and scoffers; and meditating on (muttering) God's Word to guard our hearts. The reward is the entire third verse. These verses reveal how you can directly apply boundaries to prevent sin from having easy access and devouring you.

Moral Boundaries: My bride and I love our kids so much that we had strong boundaries in their lives when they were young. And they didn't always like them! They couldn't go wherever they wanted. I'm confident those boundaries kept them alive and away from situations that could have scarred them for life. You and I may not like all of God's moral laws, but they serve individuals, churches, and nations well. God is perfect. Every law He maps out is designed to aim us toward our greater good. God is unlike an angry dad who lays down arbitrary rules to serve himself. God's laws, precepts, and teachings are given by a good Father who is glorified when we taste joy and satisfaction from Him.

Relational Boundaries: Bad company can be destructive (see 1 Cor. 15:33). Who you surround yourself with matters. Relational boundaries are not barriers that close out the world; they are protection from people who can devour what is good and feed what is destructive. People are like an elevator—they either take you up or down. Just because someone attends a church or claims to be a Christian doesn't mean they will help move you closer to God. Look at your life and those around you. Be someone for whom others don't have to set boundaries and surround yourself with people who take you up and toward God. Relational boundaries keep fools, mockers, and scoffers from stealing seeds of life from you before they have a chance to grow. The goal is not to build walls to keep people out but to build strength in your soul to ultimately help others. This is most important when you're conquering "the one thing." People who tend to feed your weakness need the most substantial boundaries. Even this can be done with grace and love. Walking alone or with a few firm friends for a season is better than surrounding yourself with destructive or diminishing relationships.

Spiritual Boundaries: When you begin to see your heart, soul, and mind as the epicenter of life, the application of truth becomes a spiritual boundary. The blessing of God flows from a guarded heart. "Above all else, guard your heart, for everything you do flows from it" (Prov. 4:23 NIV). We do this by meditating on (muttering) God's truth. The spoken and applied truth of God's Word establishes boundaries against deception and lies, flawed world systems, and our fleshly thoughts. Spiritual boundaries are unseen and cultivated in our secret places with God. Being active in a church where truth is spoken, studying Scripture, memorizing truth, and talking with God about His Word cultivate boundaries around our hearts—protecting you from being devoured by lies.

The Rewards: Boundaries bring rewards—lots of them! The things you most desire are realized from good boundaries: our thirst for something more is satisfied, our lives get stronger, we bear fruit, and the spiritual prosperity we hoped for is realized. God set before the nation of Israel a choice: "I have set before you life and death, blessing and curse. Therefore choose life" (Deut. 30:19). Pursuing the rewards of God is a worthy aim!

Starve Sin

I love feeding birds at our home. We have feeders in our front and backyard. When I refill empty feeders, I see something remarkable. A single bird flies in. At first, it's tentative. Maybe they can't believe they're all alone at the birdseed buffet, or they're just a scout for more. But then it happens: what looks like a squadron of birds descends out of nowhere, and the frenzy is on. I'll never understand how those tiny creations of God can eat so much, but in a few days, three large feeders are empty, and the birds are gone.

If we keep giving sin even the slightest amount of our affection, attention, or gratification, it will stick around, and it will kill us.

Here's a life lesson to always remember. Whatever you feed seems to keep coming back. Birds, kids, neighbors, squirrels—anything we feed never seems to leave. The same is true of sin. If we keep giving sin even the slightest amount of our affection, attention, or gratification, it will stick around, and it will kill us.

The one thing you can never stop doing is repenting. Repentance is a loving invitation by God to turn back to Him, and the celebration of repentance is enormous. Jesus said, "I tell you, there is joy before the angels of God over one sinner who repents" (Luke 15:10).

Repentance is a discipline of every strong disciple of Jesus as long as they live. It means to turn around. Repentance starves the sin of affection, attention, and gratification. Turning your back to sin starves it of the things it needs to survive. Stop feeding sin, and it will stop killing you!

Here are a few examples of specific ways to block sin:

- If you make purchases impulsively, devise creative ways to make them more challenging. For example, do not carry credit cards or, as one person I know does, have a trusted friend look at your spending ledgers for a few months. Force yourself to put space between opportunity and decision.
- If you're trying to curb your appetite, get healthy, or lose weight, avoid having foods in your kitchen that tempt you to overindulge.
- If wine, beer, hard liquor, or drugs are owning you, get them out of easy reach, distance yourself from company that causes you to stumble, and get trusted friends to pray for you and support you.
- If social media or TV are devouring your time, limit your electronics. Give passcodes to a spouse or friend. A device doesn't only give you access to the world; it gives the world access to you.

Get creative, be bold, and take action. The discipline of turning our backs to sin is practical and powerful. I've seen hundreds of people conquer sin by simply turning to God, turning their backs to sin, and building a life with quite radical boundaries that God rewards.

Whatever that one thing is, God will never call you to turn your back on something without a plan to pull it off. God will give you great wisdom when you ask. Listening closely to the Spirit guide me in truth has been the single best way to know what to turn my back on and how. God seems to give me unconventional solutions for challenging situations, and He will do the same for you.

KILL SIN—
Reflection and Application

What is a boundary that has brought rewards into your life?

Which of the three boundaries (Moral, Relational, Spiritual) do you need to improve the most and why? What practical steps can you take to block sin in that area?

What new boundaries do you need to put in place in your life to kill sin? Be specific.

Free devotional series on
the three boundaries

THAT NEXT THING

The moment had come for me to experience what my dad had been raving about. Dad had a way of describing things that built anticipation, and I was pumped up! This was my day—my time. We pulled slowly into a parking space, and Dad turned off the car. I scanned the huge A&W menu board in front of us, and there it was—this was going to happen.

A young woman on roller skates soon glided up to Dad's window. "What will it be, sir?" she asked Dad. "Root beers for both of us," Dad said with gusto. "Would you like a kiddie size for your son?" she inquired. I grew an inch with what came next. "Oh no," said Dad, "give us two large root beers!" She skated away, and Dad just smiled at me.

She soon returned with two frosted, heavy glass mugs overflowing with root beer. Dad handed me mine, and we both carefully unsheathed our straws and plunged them in. Dad began to drink, and a look of satisfaction came over his face. I stared into my chilled root beer and tried to suck up some for myself, but nothing happened. I sucked harder still, only managing to pull up what seemed to be atomized specks of root beer. It was at that point I first learned about "cracked straw syndrome." I had a barely visible crack in my straw just above the root beer line.

Killing sin is not a book to read; it is a life to live.

We have cracks of sin in our spiritual lives that make it impossible to drink deeply of the liberating life God offers us. We're born with these cracks and acquire more along the way. These sin cracks are often easily seen but sometimes barely visible to those looking on. More sin cracks will appear, but you now have the biblical plan and tools to conquer the sin that is defeating you.

Killing sin is not a book to read; it is a life to live. I'm so glad you read this book; it shows you take sin seriously. But stay alert and engaged in conquering what's defeating you. You probably came to this book with multiple sins you could identify, and there are more you'll discover along the way. My purpose was to demonstrate that God can handle our biggest messes, give us a taste of victory, and grant us a vision for conquering that next thing. Please take a moment to celebrate God's work in your life. Killing sin is an ongoing discipline of conquering those things that are killing you.

My dad, Joseph Clauson, who went home to his reward at the age of ninety-five, often recited with gusto, "And I am sure of this, that he who began a good work in you will bring it to completion at the day of Jesus Christ" (Phil. 1:6). I am sure as well!

It's never too late, and you're never too old. You're never too worn out or too worn down. You're never too lost or too far gone. You're never too battered or shattered for God to pull it all together.

God can do more through your frailty than you can ever pull off through all your ingenuity, will, and strength. If you can take a breath, you have a life that needs to be fully lived.

Stories that will inspire you **to kill sin**

GOING FURTHER

Where You Go from Here
and How We Can Help

My deepest desire is for you to experience God's power, conquer sin, and thrive as a disciple of Christ. My team and I want to come alongside you and provide practical resources to help you conquer that one thing that is defeating you. The following resources are available at KillSin.com.

Because killing sin is a life to live, I want to provide you with a *free devotional series* that will further help you put to death those sins that have been killing you. This devotional series will also help you imagine experiencing other promises of God, which I cover in my previous book, *The 7 Resolutions: Where Self-Help Ends and God's Power Begins*:

- You are partnering with God and experiencing His power.
- Your mind is being renewed and freed from destructive thinking.
- You have quality people around you who help you live the abundant life.
- You now live in a way that puts your faith in motion and gives you energy.

- Your direction is clear because you're focused on your passion and gifting.
- You're making the best use of your time and impacting the world.

Simply scan this QR code below, and you'll know exactly where to go from here and how we can help. I'm grateful you have the courage to face the sin that's defeating you and dare to believe God can conquer it—Godspeed!

What Scriptures to Speak Into Your Life and Over Your Sin (Starter Guide)

God's Word is our offensive weapon of war. When the truth of God's Word is at work in your life, it gives you solid footing and a sword to conquer the sin that's defeating you. I've provided Scriptures for specific areas of sin and essential truth for your identity and victory in Christ. You may want to commit some of these to memory or write them on notecards.

The goal is to hide God's Word in your heart so you can renew your mind and speak the truth during battle. This is a starter guide, and I pray that you find many more truths to wield as you conquer what's defeating you and fend off future battles.

Greed
Proverbs 28:25
Matthew 6:19–21
Matthew 6:24
2 Corinthians 9:6–8
1 Timothy 6:6–10
1 John 3:16–18

Anger
Psalm 37:8
Proverbs 14:29
Proverbs 16:32
Matthew 5:21–24
Ephesians 4:26
James 1:19–20

Pride/Self-Righteousness
Proverbs 11:2
Romans 12:16
2 Corinthians 10:17–18
Ephesians 2:8–10
Philippians 2:3–4

Lust
Matthew 5:27–30
1 Corinthians 6:18–20
Galatians 5:19–21
1 Thessalonians 4:3–8
1 John 2:16

Laziness
Proverbs 14:23
Proverbs 19:15
Ephesians 5:15–17
Colossians 3:23–24
2 Thessalonians 3:10–12

Envy/Jealousy
Psalm 37:1–2
Proverbs 14:30
James 3:13–16
James 4:1–4
1 John 2:15–17

Gluttony
Psalms 78:18
Proverbs 23:20–21
1 Corinthians 6:12
Galatians 5:16
Philippians 3:18–19

Gossip
Exodus 23:1
Leviticus 19:16
Psalms 34:13
Ephesians 4:29
James 4:11–12

People-Pleasing
Proverbs 29:25
Luke 12:8–12
John 15:18–20
Galatians 1:9–10
1 Thessalonians 2:3–6

Resentment/Bitterness
Proverbs 19:11
Matthew 7:1–5
Ephesians 4:31–32
Hebrews 12:14–15
1 John 2:9–11

Unforgiveness
Matthew 6:14–15
Mark 11:25
Luke 17:3–4
Ephesians 4:32
Colossians 3:12–13

ESSENTIAL TRUTH FOR YOUR IDENTITY AND VICTORY IN CHRIST

Romans 8:13–17

1 Corinthians 10:13

Galatians 2:20

Galatians 3:2–6

Philippians 4:5–8

Colossians 3:2–10

Titus 2:11–14

James 1:22–24

1 Peter 1:13–16

1 Peter 3:8–12

2 Peter 1:3–8

1 John 1:5–10

How to Deal with Sin in Others

One of the best relationship tools I ever received was the Drama Triangle, which Stephen Karpman first described in the 1960s. This model of dysfunctional relational interactions illustrates three corners you need to stay out of when someone isn't ready to conquer their sin: Victim, Rescuer, and Persecutor. Each of these is a typical but ineffective response to people who are unable or unwilling to face and conquer what's defeating them.[12]

DRAMA TRIANGLE

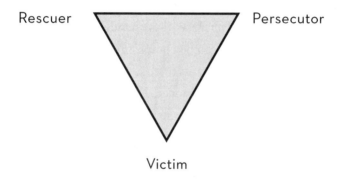

Rescuer   Persecutor

Victim

This book is primarily about dealing with and killing our sins. But we also must grapple with how to deal with others' sins. These can be divided into three main categories: (1) those who sin against us, (2) those who are stuck in sinful patterns but desire to repent and kill their sin, and (3) those who are stuck in sinful patterns but don't view it as sin or don't want to repent.

In the first category, there are those who sin against us. Their sin causes hurt and pain. If we are not careful, unforgiveness and bitterness can fester. Running to one or more of the three corners is tempting in response to that hurt and pain. Depending on your proximity to that person, it may be right for you to share with them the pain you experienced without running to a corner that will only exacerbate or prolong the hurt or pain.

Secondly, some are stuck in sinful patterns but desire to repent and kill their sin. This may be a loved one or close brother or sister in Christ who is overcome with sin and struggling to break free. Though they desire freedom and acknowledge their sin, we must resist the temptation to run to the **Rescuer** or **Persecutor** corners. This gets in God's way and can delay God's work in their life.

Finally, there are those who are stuck in sinful patterns but don't see it as sin or don't want to repent and conquer it. Either they are blind to what they are doing, or they haven't yet come to the end of themselves. If we don't handle them rightly, our joy and journey with God can be compromised. But we can also get in the way of what God wants to do in their lives. Again, it can be tempting to head off to **Rescuer**, **Persecutor**, or **Victim** mode, but you must stay out of these corners.

You might find yourself in a destructive relationship. It may be that you can't get distance from this person because you are married to them, or they are a family member or coworker that involves proximity. We all need to understand how relationships get trapped in these corners and why we need to stay out of them.

VICTIM—We can all identify someone who hurt or injured us. Stepping out of the victim corner does not minimize the offense or the pain. But stepping out of the corner finally allows us to breathe and live. Being a victim of someone's sin is painful, but living as a victim is a tragic way to live. Despite everything that batters us, we are "more than conquerors through him who loved us" (Rom. 8:31–37).

RESCUER—When we step into this corner, we can preempt what God is trying to do in the other person. Often, we see our role as needing to save a person who is floundering and failing. But only God can save someone from their sin. We simply can't get in God's way. We ought to come alongside and assist however we can to help others in their battle against sin, but it is ultimately God who saves and rescues. We don't want anyone to miss the ultimate Rescuer who "came into the world to save sinners" (1 Tim. 1:15).

PERSECUTOR—This corner provides some cheap relief but no satisfaction. The main reason not to go here is to allow God to deal with people from His vantage point and in His time. We expend valuable energy and time trying to be the hand of justice. This is the ultimate trap. There is zero justice or justification for playing the persecutor. We must leave room for God to do His work. "Vengeance is mine, I will repay" (Rom. 12:19). This doesn't mean we are silent about others' sin. Sin is serious and has consequences. We speak the truth in love without being the judge, jury, and executioner.

VICTORY TRIANGLE

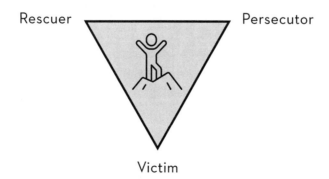

Rescuer · Persecutor

Victim

The chart above is my application of the Drama Triangle in light of how God has saved us and is training us. We are positioned in power when our feet are firmly planted in Christ alone. If you never stand in these three corners, you have the best hope of seeing people conquer what's defeating them, and you stand to thrive in Christ!

ACKNOWLEDGMENTS

Many thanks to some special people. Shawn McDuffee, you put this book proposal together—it wouldn't have begun without you. Drew Dyck, your optimism and encouragement in acquiring and launching *Killing Sin* fueled my soul. Ajit and Katie Christopher, the hard work of structuring content to make this book compelling and clear was terrific. Connor Sterchi, your heart for God and people shone brightly as you painstakingly made recommendations and edited the manuscript. Lori Ridder, you're the best Executive Assistant a pastor could possibly have—you keep the trains running on time. And to all those who worked in proofreading, promotions, and advertising and who work at KillSin.com, a big shout-out of appreciation. Prayer is the engine room of God's power, and my bride of thirty-seven years, Junanne Clauson, has been in prayer for me, the team, and this entire project. Thanks to you, Babe.

NOTES

1. John Owen, *On Temptation and the Mortification of Sin in Believers* (Philadelphia: Presbyterian Board of Publication, 1855), 154.

2. Owen, *Mortification of Sin*, 291.

3. *Merriam-Webster Dictionary*, "momentum," last updated October 14, 2024, https://www.merriam-webster.com/dictionary/momentum.

4. James Clear, *Atomic Habits: An Easy & Proven Way to Build Good Habits & Break Bad Ones* (New York: Penguin, 2018), 27.

5. John Stott, "Pride, Humility, and God," in J. I. Packer and Loren Wilkinson, eds., *Alive to God: Studies in Spirituality* (Downers Grove, IL: InterVarsity Press, 1992), 119.

6. Andrew Murray, *Humility: The Beauty of Holiness* (London: James Nisbet & Co., 1896), 14.

7. "Why Is There Liberty Where the Spirit of the Lord Is (2 Corinthians 3:17)?," Got Questions, https://www.gotquestions.org/Spirit-of-the-Lord-liberty.html.

8. "Psalm 32—The Blessings of Forgiveness, Protection, and Guidance," Enduring Word, https://enduringword.com/bible-commentary/psalm-32/.

9. Erwin Lutzer, *Failure: The Back Door to Success* (Chicago: Moody Publishers, 2015), 52.

10. Owen, *Mortification of Sin*, 154.

11. John Piper, "Kill Sin by the Spirit," Desiring God, February 17, 2002, https://www.desiringgod.org/messages/kill-sin-by-the-spirit.

12. "The Drama Triangle Explained," Leadership Tribe, https://leadershiptribe.com/the-drama-triangle-explained/.

∧
T7R

COACHING

Are you ready to say no to self-help and yes to God's power?

Is there a gap between God's promise of abundant life and your own daily experience?

Have you grown accustomed to bad habits, written off lifelong battles as unwinnable?

Do you believe that some destructive behaviors can never be changed?

We want to help you close that gap.
You don't have to settle for too little.
The time is now for humble dependence on God
and a plan to walk in His power!

Sign up now for our free devotional on how
you can walk in the victory God has promised.